# THE FIXER

THE
FIXER

# THE FIXER

forging unstoppable teams

## TAUNI CREFELD

**MIL.SPACE BOOKS**

an imprint of W. Brand Publishing

NASHVILLE, TENNESSEE

Copyright ©2025 Tauni Crefeld

*The views and opinions expressed in this book are those of the author and do not necessarily reflect the official policy or position of W. Brand Publishing.*

All rights reserved. No part of this publication may be reproduced, distributed or transmitted in any form or by any means, including photocopying, recording, or other electronic or mechanical methods, without the prior written permission of the publisher, except in the case of brief quotations embodied in critical reviews and certain other noncommercial uses permitted by copyright law.

j.brand@wbrandpub.com

MilSpace Books

www.wbrandpub.com

Cover design by JuLee Brand / designchik

*The Fixer* / Tauni Crefeld —1st ed.

Available in Paperback, eBook and Kindle formats.

Paperback ISBN: **979-8-89503-004-2**

eBook ISBN: **979-8-89503-005-9**

Library of Congress Control Number: 2024924325

# CONTENTS

1. Forging Unstoppable Teams: Project Falcon Case Study ............ 1
   - Leading with the Team ............ 3
   - The Right People in the Right Roles ............ 12
   - Troops Eat First: The Leader Is Only as Good as Their Team ............ 19
   - Two-Dimensional Leadership ............ 23
   - The Third Dimension ............ 34
   - You Can't Fix It Alone ............ 37
   - Strong Teams: Summary ............ 39
2. One Objective to Rule Them All: Project Ascend Case Study .. 43
   - One Team ............ 44
   - Level the Playing Field ............ 50
   - More on the WHAT ............ 57
   - Where There Is a Morale Problem ............ 60
   - Listen, Listen, Listen ............ 68
   - Bully Culture and Other Challenging Cultures ............ 74
   - No Blame; Just Solutions ............ 78
   - What Is a Strong Team ............ 92
3. Fast but Not Furious: Project Blast Case Study ............ 97
   - The Right People ............ 99
   - Critical Thinking: Reverse Jeopardy ............ 102
   - Wherever You Can Best Lead ............ 105
   - The Accountability and Commitment Trap ............ 107
   - Just Solutions ............ 110
   - Project Blast Summary ............ 115
4. Large Organizations: Project Nebula Case Study ............ 121
   - Relationships ............ 128
   - Dealing with Difficult People ............ 141
   - Intentional Communications ............ 148
   - Asking for Help ............ 157
5. Managing Your Career ............ 167
   - Why Move Up? ............ 167
   - Level the Career Playing Field ............ 187
   - Networking ............ 197
   - Taking and Giving Credit ............ 200
   - Giving Feedback ............ 204
6. Last Points ............ 215
   - Remote Work ............ 215
   - Take Care of Yourself ............ 221
7. Summary ............ 227
8. Appendix ............ 229
9. End Notes ............ 233
10. Author Bio ............ 235

1.

# FORGING UNSTOPPABLE TEAMS: PROJECT FALCON CASE STUDY

My boss called me and asked, "What do you know about Project Falcon?"

"Isn't that the project that Max is leading?" I asked.

"Yes, what do you know about it?"

"Nothing." I hesitated, "Except . . . I heard it's not going well, and the team is miserable."

"I need you to fix it," he said.

Project Falcon was a large software development program that my company was leading. I was being nice when I said it wasn't going well. From what I had heard, it sounded like a black hole of misery. The team was burned out. Everyone said to avoid it.

The project was plummeting, and I was being asked (Told!) to pull the team out of the death spiral.

I had led a lot of strong teams in my career, starting in the military, and then during twelve years in my consulting firm. In fact, I had just finished leading a project in which I guided three disparate companies through the setup and national rollout of an extremely complex new cloud technology. This wasn't my first goat rodeo.

But this would be new for me. I'd never fixed a broken team, and this one sounded as messy and awful as they come. To make things harder, I had just been promoted to the executive level, and the people leading the project had until recently been my peers. It was going to feel strange to walk in and take over the project. I also didn't know anything about the software we were building, never having worked on either system being built.

I asked my boss, "What about Max?"

He said, "Don't overthink it. Just go fix it."

*Oh, is that all?* I thought. *Just fix it.*

It wasn't the first time I'd had to walk in and be the boss. I'd had a similar experience as a new lieutenant in the military, after having graduated from the United States Air Force Academy.

That first leadership role taught me how to lead a team, build relationships, and leverage the team's experience; that was going to be crucial on Project Falcon, since I didn't have experience in the technologies my team was supposed to build. And I couldn't just waltz in and tell this team of my former peers what to do. In fact, I was going to have to leverage *all* my experience from both the military and the consulting company where I'd worked for the past years.

I'm not going to tell you it was easy. I'm not going to tell you there were "three simple steps" or any BS like that. Anyone who tells you there are simple rules for leadership hasn't been a real boots-on-the-ground leader. Or they don't really understand their team and what their team is going through.

Leadership is messy; building strong teams takes dedication and hard work, and there is no single formula that works. There are principles you can apply, but the leader will need to listen, learn, adapt, and continue to work with the team, for the team, and until the team is as strong as they should be.

I knew how to lead strong teams; I'd been leading them my whole career. But only when I walked into a broken team and had to repair it did I really start to understand some of the factors that can break (or make) a team.

This "recovery" project (which is just a nicer way to describe a broken project, or a project that needed to be fixed), a few other key projects, and the lessons I learned through each of them will be the focus of the book.

I will tell you the unvarnished truth of what I had to go through, so you can also learn some of the principles I used to build strong teams, many of which may also be useful to you.

Hopefully, you'll also learn a few things *not* to do, because let's be honest, I didn't get everything right along the way.

But first, let me back up and help you understand who I am, and how I got to the point where my boss would think I could handle fixing Project Falcon, even though I'd never done it before. I'll also tell you the hard-fought leadership lessons that I had to apply to make Project Falcon work.

## LEADING *WITH* THE TEAM

My first leadership lessons came from the military, especially about how to learn from the team and still be able to lead it, a delicate balance. While many leadership books and movies show hard-as-nails leaders who make snap decisions, set the direction, and push the team, that was not my experience of leadership in real life.

The Air Force Academy, like all of the other service academies (including West Point for Army or the Naval Academy), serves as a leadership laboratory. New cadets (called "basic cadets") go through a basic training course in the summer to learn the ropes of military life, including how to wear a uniform, make a bed, keep a room at inspection-level cleanliness, how to march, how to salute, and how to shoot a weapon. We had to run an obstacle course, plus an assault course, which is an obstacle course you run while carrying an old, heavy wooden weapon and being yelled at. The leaders who are responsible for these incoming basic cadets are the third- and fourth-year students who are acting like the sergeants or officers, preparing for their own careers as leaders as they train incoming newbies.

Every cadet who graduates grows through these stages of leadership, from basic cadet to senior cadet to officer, something like what you see on those T-shirts showing the evolution from ape to man.

Another rite of passage for cadets is choosing your career field (or military job), which for most of my classmates was "pilot," but there are other specialties in the Air Force like intelligence, maintenance, and logistics. Since I was not pilot-qualified due to my lack of 20/20 vision, I had to make a choice.

My father had been in the Air Force, so I asked for his guidance. He said, "Whatever you do, don't choose security police. They eat their young."

I chose security police.

I didn't do it to defy him (I don't think!). I chose it because it would mean that I could lead troops and be as much of a leader as the military would allow me to be. Females were restricted from combat roles at the time.

After graduation, I was sent to my first duty station, in Grand Forks, North Dakota, to be a missile field flight leader. I would be responsible for guarding America's nuclear weapons. When I arrived in Grand Forks, I was given a flight of forty airmen (Air Force soldiers), and the only experience

I had was my Air Force Academy leadership lessons and a week of training, riding along with a seasoned lieutenant.

I was twenty-one but I looked younger than that, and I had been a real officer for about a week. I was 5'4," slim, and looked like I was being swallowed by my battle dress uniform (BDU), with its camouflage cargo pants and a multi-pocket button up shirt, which was designed for men but shrunk to, kind of, fit women.

I was working with enlisted troops, some of whom had a whole career under their belts, who had families and responsibilities outside of work. They were also all men, and all but two of them were older than me. Two young, enlisted women were added into my flight after I joined.

Despite my Air Force Academy leadership training, or perhaps partly because of it, I had images in my mind of General Patton leading his troops, the same way you probably do from having watched military movies. But the problem is, that's not real life. Yes, I was "in charge." Yes, I was the officer, and yes, my troops had to salute me. But, in reality I was twenty-one and didn't know anything. I probably kept the Patton image in my head for all of a day before I realized it just wasn't going to work for me.

As missile field security, our job was to live in Launch Control Facilities (LCFs) in the missile field and protect and defend the missiles from any threat to them. This meant that we lived for half of the week in the missile field and the other half of the week at home. In the missile field, even when I was "off" from my twelve-hour shift, I was still living in the LCF with troops who were both on and off duty.

As the officer, I still had to be "on." My troops were watching me, and I felt like they were judging me, so I wanted to hold myself to a high standard.

After I dropped the image of Patton, I might say I tried to "build relationships" with the troops, but I don't think it was that conscious. I just knew that if I wanted to have any impact with them, I had to get along with them, and I had to understand where they were coming from. So, I did what I could to build their trust in me and get along, while still trying to be professional.

I started to notice that every time I walked in on a group of soldiers talking, if one of them dropped a curse word (which was a frequent occurrence), they always stopped and said, "Pardon me, LT." This not only called attention to me, but made them nervous to keep talking casually. I tried to put them at ease by saying, "I don't mind." Or, "You don't have to say that," but it had no effect. They all continued to pardon themselves in front of me. So, I changed it up and said, "Oh, for fuck's sake, I don't give a shit if you swear."

After I started swearing *with* my soldiers, I was able to get them to confide in me, take me under their wing, and teach me about the real world they worked in. I never swore *at* people, and I never swore in anger. I built real and lasting relationships with those soldiers, some of whom I'm still in close contact with today. Eventually, I was able to be an effective leader and mentor for them. They came to me when they wanted me to take a request to the leadership or to defend them against the facility managers. If I'd have continued to beat my chest and act like Patton, I never would have gotten there.

I kept swearing in the civilian world, and it was a good tool for me. I used it to disarm tension and make people feel like they could confide in me by reducing formality and bringing down barriers. Swearing became a way of getting closer to people, and it worked for me.

Beyond swearing, I started building a relationship with everyone on the team, most especially the senior sergeants, who were my right-hand men and women and who were teaching me the ropes, if I was smart enough to listen.

I also built camaraderie by pulling pranks like the sergeants did. They were mild by the standards of military pranks. My favorite was something I did when we returned from being on the road. As the sergeant and I walked into the LFC, I would say, "Your lights are off," and the sergeant would always turn back to check his lights. Worked every time.

We dealt with each situation that arose by working as a team, me learning from the sergeants and learning how to pull my weight. Together, we became a stronger team and I became accepted as its leader.

I'll highlight a couple of stories to illustrate the kinds of situations my team encountered and how we handled them by working together. North Dakota in the winter is brutal. To those of you who are trying to get to all fifty states, don't go to North Dakota in the winter. Once my team was driving between LCFs when a white-out blizzard hit us. In North Dakota, out in the missile fields there is a whole lot of nothing. No trees, no houses, no landmarks, no mountains. It is flat, and when the land is covered with white, and the sky is white, and the road is white, there is nothing by which to navigate. The sergeant was driving and told me to open my door and stick my head out and tell him where the white line was. We were probably only going 10 miles an hour. I don't know how long we had to do that; it felt like forever. But together we made it to the LCF.

Another time we encountered a pickup that had rolled over in a ditch, and the driver was lying beside it. He was conscious, but it was in the days before cell phones, so we radioed to get our dispatch to call the local police and ambulance. We stayed with him and kept him talking and warm until the local squads arrived. Fortunately, this didn't happen during a blizzard. But even in a North Dakota summer it can get cold, and if you're in shock and help doesn't come along, it could be bad.

Days like those were when I became part of the team, not just the lieutenant. I got to participate in the war stories over dinner instead of just listening.

To be a leader, you have to figure out how to lead *within* an organization, and within the context of that organization. You need to figure out what you bring and who you can be for the team. You'll need to spend time to understand the team and the mission before you can understand how best to lead *with* them.

I led units from forty up to two hundred and loved military leadership. I left as a captain after five years of service, because as one progresses in the security police career field the journey takes you away from hands-on leadership and toward back-office and policy work. I wanted to stay a hands-on leader, as that was where I felt truly alive and where I had the most to give.

After I left the military, I joined one of the major consulting companies, without really knowing what they did. I had a broad engineering education from the Air Force Academy, but it was seven years outdated. While my military leadership experience would be helpful eventually, my five years of toting a gun in the military didn't count for much in the civilian world.

But I needed a job, and my company saw something in me and gave me a chance, although I didn't really fit the profile of a new joiner at the time. Most of the new joiners were twenty-two years old and straight out of college, and the company "grew" each new batch of entry-level workers through on-the-job training. I went into that same batch of entry-level newbies, what we called "analysts."

Moving into the civilian sector was a rude awakening. I couldn't take the same confidence I'd had in the military and apply it to the civilian world. I had been a captain, a respected rank, in the Air Force, responsible for leading troops and protecting our military assets and personnel. I was saluted, called "ma'am," and acknowledged as a leader.

When I joined my consulting company, I was nothing more than a grunt, an "individual contributor," not a leader. My first role was to perform testing on a UNIX-based client-server ordering site for a telecom company. If none of those words mean anything to you, don't worry. They meant nothing to me at the time, either. I had to learn everything from the bottom up, and the only way to do that was to ask and to listen and learn quickly. It was 1998, before Google and before the rise of the Internet, so I couldn't just Google for the meaning of various UNIX commands.

While my general engineering background was helpful to my job (in terms of helping me understand quickly), the Air Force at the time was not advanced in technology, at least not in the security police career field. It was only during the last few months of my five-years of service that we got email. Just three years earlier, my dispatchers in North Dakota had still been keeping their event logs on typewriters. Yes, typewriters.

So, when I joined my consulting firm, and was given email and a voicemail box, and everything was online . . . I realized how far behind I was. During orientation, we were learning how to do time reports on laptops, and I had to ask where the mouse was. (It was a track ball built into the keyboard, and I'd never seen one.)

I wasn't in charge any longer. I didn't have any troops, and once again, I didn't have any knowledge. I started doing the same thing I'd done in the military—listening, learning, and building relationships.

After a year, I was given a team of four to lead. It felt so puny, so insignificant compared to the teams I'd lead in the past, but the work we were doing was very different.

In the military I was able to be almost solely focused on my troops, their needs, and their problems. There wasn't a lot of creativity with the mission we were doing, as we were walking over well-trodden ground of executing the mission.

On the other hand, my team of four was tasked with creating something, with developing a system to solve a problem. This meant there was a different level of problem-solving required. And I had to lead this team to do it. I couldn't just tell the team to do it; they didn't know what to do either. We had to figure it out together, with me as the leader, understanding each of my team members' skills and how best to utilize their talents to get us to the right result. For example, I learned that one team member was stronger with the technical aspects of the project, so I had him focus on our interfaces. Meanwhile, another team member was stronger with communication, so I had him write the instructions on using the system that we would give to our clients.

As I progressed in my career in consulting, I chose or was assigned to projects that allowed me to lead larger and larger teams, and my skill with leading teams grew.

For those of you unfamiliar with consulting, companies hire consultants when they need either skills or manpower they don't have in-house. The consultants then set up a team to do whatever the company needs. The teams can be very small or very large, or individual consultants may even augment a company's staff. Sometimes, the projects are short-term, lasting a few weeks or a few months, or they could span multiple years. I've played the single-consultant role, and I've led teams from four to two hundred. I've been on short projects that lasted just a few weeks, and I stayed at one company for seven years, so long that my clients all but forgot I wasn't their employee.

The team of consultants works within the larger environment or culture of the company that hired them. The consultants are effectively a team within the company team, and those teams have to work together well, the way different gears have to work together in a machine. Where the teams work together well, the machine works well, and the project gets done. If there is friction between teams, or broken teams (like broken gears), the machine doesn't work well, and it's a lot harder to get the project completed.

The other thing with consulting is most consultants will work with many corporations. I worked in around twenty different corporate environments during my career, and in each one I had to learn the corporate culture and corporate team structure in order to make my consulting team work within the larger team.

There are also, of course, competing consulting firms who would often be in the same environment, setting up their own teams at the request of the company, adding more complexity and more gears into the machine.

As a fixer, my job was often stepping in to understand what had broken down in the machine, whether the problems were in the consulting team, in the client environment, or in the interaction between the two. Usually, it was a combination of all of those factors, and I had to work with the teams to get them resolved and get the machine working again.

Because as a consultant I had to set up, run, or fix so many teams within numerous corporate environments, I gained a lot of experience leading teams—much more than I could have gotten in a single corporate environment. Being a consultant leading teams was in many ways like living in a leadership laboratory, one in which millions of dollars and the corporate goals and careers of my clients, myself, and my bosses were on the line.

In all the teams I built, I stayed focused on the team itself and the work we were supposed to do. That focus helped make the teams strong and harmonious, and it ended up producing better results. I applied a lot of lessons from the military, leveraging my experience and what I knew had worked for me.

## THE RIGHT PEOPLE IN THE RIGHT ROLES

If I was going to take over Project Falcon, I couldn't walk in like Patton and beat my chest and tell the team what to do. First of all, I didn't know what was going wrong. So even if I'd wanted to come in like Patton, I wouldn't have known what to tell them.

I couldn't ask the team's former leader, Max, what was going wrong. Would he even know? Would whatever he told me be even remotely accurate? Clearly, he was out of touch as a leader and had no idea how to fix things. That is, if the project truly was as big a pit of misery as the rumors claimed.

The only approach that seemed to make sense was the same one I'd used in the military. I'd have to learn from the team what was going on and then figure out where the challenges were. I'd have to learn about the mission and what the team needed to be successful. I'd have to build relationships and tackle each issue until the chaos was turned into order and the team was strong enough to handle the mission.

The first thing I did on Project Falcon was start talking to the team. One at a time, I pulled people into my office and asked, "How's it going?" I spoke to senior people, as well as more junior team members and technical people working across both pieces of the software we were supposed to develop.

It felt like every individual had been just dropped out of the sky onto the team. Many of the people had generally the right skills, but there hadn't been a lot of leadership and follow-up to make sure that the person had the right experience, support, or direction. They weren't gelled as a team and they didn't all know what they were supposed to be doing. Some people were underutilized and some were way overutilized. Everyone was getting yelled at and told they weren't doing a good job.

One person that exemplified the problem was Andrew, a young new joiner straight out of college. He was doing whatever was asked of him, task by task, but he hadn't been given anything to own and sink his teeth into. He was busy all day long, but . . . what was he accomplishing? He was frustrated and was questioning whether the consulting company was right for him. We were getting about 50 percent of his value, and we were going to lose that if we didn't give him something to own.

I spent a lot of time with the two most senior people on the project, not including Max, who was getting transitioned out, a delivery leader named Chris, and a project manager named John. Chris, the delivery leader, was supposed to be in charge of the whole team, and John, the project manager, was supposed to manage the schedule and be aware of all of the detailed tasks, risks, and issues.

Chris and John were in every meeting together, and they couldn't seem to operate independently. They didn't seem to be doing either of their jobs well. There wasn't a detailed project plan to get the work done, and the whole team was working hard but no one knew where they were going. It was like there was a whole bunch of people chopping trees every day, but I wasn't sure if everyone was in the same forest, and I'm not sure everyone knew what they were trying to do. How many trees did we need to chop to be done?

I separated Chris and John to see what they knew independently and to determine whether either could be trained up to serve their individual role well.

Chris, the delivery leader, was a good guy but he had never delivered a project like this. He was a good relationship person, developing strong loyalties with his clients, but he was not a technical delivery leader and didn't understand the details of the project. He didn't understand all of the steps his team needed to take to get the work done. The project had gotten away from him, and he had been hiding behind the project manager, John.

I tried to see if Chris could be used elsewhere on the project, but given that his role had been top dog, moving him to another role would have been awkward for him and for the team, so I rolled him off. ("Rolling off" is the consulting term for "leaving a project," but anyone who is rolled off is still employed and can just move to a different project.)

I brought on a new delivery leader who had done this kind of work before, and he became my right-hand man.

Meanwhile, John was organized and had the energy to be a good project manager, but he had never created a project plan for a team like this and it was over his head. John was frankly resistant to our coaching. He was in denial about how messy the project was, and he still thought either that things had been going well and he had it under control, or that even if the project hadn't been going well, he was personally still doing great. The new delivery leader and I sat with him and worked through a detailed project plan.

We poured a lot of energy into getting him upskilled and the project plan built, and then he quit the company. I think he assumed his performance reviews would be impacted that year, and, of course, he still believed that he was an amazing performer and didn't take any responsibility for the challenges on the team—so he left.

We were so much better once John was gone. Anytime there is such a stark mismatch between someone's view of their own skills and accomplishments and the actual results they're achieving, they will continue to underperform and continue to be challenging to coach. Why should they improve if they think they're amazing already?

Rather than bringing on a new project manager, we gave the project plan to Andrew, the new joiner who was underchallenged, and worked with him to take on the role. Andrew thrived on having something to own and blossomed from being "task guy" to being a full-fledged project manager, and we were so happy with his performance that he was promoted that year.

The whole team was like that . . . some people were underutilized, like Andrew, and once we "grew them" into a bigger role or into the right role, they flourished. And there were people like John and Chris, who just didn't have the right skills and were getting by or hiding. I had to go through the whole team and either upskill them, shift them to a different role, or replace them.

It was slow going, since the team had to keep churning out code while I was making improvements to the team. By the end of the year, there were only a handful of original members on the team in their original roles.

## roll them off

"Roll them off and let them be effective somewhere else." It's a phrase I've used dozens of times. It can sound dismissive, sarcastic, or like a euphemism for kicking someone off the team. But . . . it is 100 percent true.

Again, "rolling off" means someone no longer works on a specific project, but they are still an employee of the company and can just "roll on" to another project. Consultants are used to moving from project to project, so rolling on and rolling off is a normal part of our lives.

However, there are multiple kinds of roll-offs. A person can be scheduled to roll off when their piece of the project has been completed, especially if their part is based on a specific skill. The whole team can roll off when the project has been completed. Or, a person can be rolled off when their skill doesn't match the need of the project, or if they're just not performing up to expectations.

The real challenge is when someone isn't performing to expectations. The first thing you should do is let the person know that they're not doing what you expected, and then explain what you wanted and why. You'll coach them on how to do the work or align them with a mentor on the program if possible. You might give them a couple of weeks with the right supervision and support, and if they still aren't performing well, you likely roll them off.

That's the way it should work.

What happens sometimes, though, is a case like Project Falcon, where the leader of the team isn't engaged enough to know what is happening, and individuals are left to struggle through roles they didn't have the skills for. Chris and John just didn't have the right skills or experience for their roles and the whole team was impacted as a result. Things started turning around after I rolled Chris off and after John quit. (I probably should have rolled John off too, but I was hopeful I could coach him up to speed, and I was wary of destabilizing the team by taking both leaders away.)

Sometimes, the leader is aware or suspects that someone may not be performing, but they're afraid of conflict. And rolling someone off is like giving a negative performance review. There is confrontation involved. The individual's feelings will usually be hurt. No one likes to hear that they aren't doing a great job.

But here's the thing: If you let them stay on the project, it hurts the project. The rest of the team will have to make up for that person's weakness and that will cause extra work or harder work. If the boss is unwilling to roll off that one person, there are likely a few other people who aren't performing to the right level, and the teams will have to cover for them as well. That will cause morale issues across the whole team, and it may also jeopardize timelines, because people will have to do more than their normal allotted work. Or it could cause the whole team to underperform, like in the case of Project Falcon.

It also ends up hurting the person whose feelings you're trying not to hurt. If a person who is struggling is left on the job, it's unlikely they will suddenly become one of your star performers. Which means that at the end of the year, when it's time for ratings and reviews, they won't get a good review, which will impact their salary and bonus, etc.

On multiple occasions, I've seen that sometimes a different role and a different project really are better for a person. If they were able to do something different, they could perform well and get a better rating at the end of the year.

So, if leaving someone in a role they aren't performing in isn't good for either the project *or* the worker, why does it still happen? If your company has flexibility in roles or positions, then not liking confrontation isn't a good enough reason to keep a person around. It's the leader's job to handle those kinds of situations for the sake of the workers and the project.

## if you can't roll off . . .
## roll over or transfer laterally

Of course, not every job has the same flexibility as consulting, and you can't just roll workers off that easily. In those cases, there may be other options, such as lateral transfers, or roll-overs, to other roles for which their skills may be better suited.

The "roll over" concept was even useful for my son, Jono. He had written a film script and gathered up a team of friends and classmates to film it. My son was a film student at the time, and since film students are not typically flush with cash, everyone on the team, mostly film students themselves, was a volunteer.

Jono came to me for advice because one of the members of his team, Steve, wasn't doing a good job as a production assistant. He was dragging his feet on finding shooting locations, and he hadn't put together a plan. Jono asked whether he should just do the work himself and how he could do that without making Steve feel bad. But Jono was running the whole film and was already overburdened, so taking over the work of one of his team members seemed like setting himself up for failure.

I said, jokingly but also realistically, that Jono should "roll him off." But Jono didn't want to take Steve off the project; they'd worked well together in the past and there also weren't that many film students available for Jono to bring onto the project.

I asked Jono what Steve was good at. Jono immediately said Steve was good at writing, filming, and being creative, which didn't line up with the role he was doing, which was more organizational and administrative. As we talked through it, I could see Jono's eyes light up and he knew it was just a mismatch of skill to role.

Jono shifted Steve to a role that fit him better and found someone else to cover the production role Steve had been doing. Steve knew he was struggling with the role but didn't want to admit it, and he was embarrassed to let Jono down. Jono was afraid to tell Steve, because he was a friend and a volunteer, and he didn't want him to quit the project.

"Rolling him over" to an alternate role made everyone happy. The new role better aligned with Steve's skills, and it let him be successful.

Likewise, on Project Falcon the biggest challenge I identified was that very few of the team members really had the skills or the experience for the jobs they were doing. They were good people—smart people—but putting an accountant in an architect's role won't yield good results, no matter how good an accountant they are. Or, having an architect who has designed houses in a role to design skyscrapers won't work either.

Recovery projects are like onions. Once you get the first layer of challenges tackled, you're able to peel back and see what else is wrong. Unfortunately, Project Falcon's former leader, Max, hadn't been engaged enough to understand the challenges or make the changes needed. On Project Falcon, getting the right people in the right roles was only the first layer. Once I'd made many changes to the team, I could see that the team still needed a lot of support and guidance to move in the right direction. Then I started to feel like I was in my element, doing the same kinds of things I did in the military, except without the guns.

## TROOPS EAT FIRST: THE LEADER IS ONLY AS GOOD AS THEIR TEAM

After I had changed out several of the major roles on Project Falcon and had the start of a stronger team, I still had a long way to go to get the team humming. The next major layer of the onion was to start supporting and guiding the team. They had been struggling for months with little or no leadership and it showed.

One of the most important lessons I'd learned in the military was that a leader's job was the team; without the team there is no need for a leader.

After the first couple of months working in my security police squadron, learning the ropes from my sergeants, the Air Force finally sent me to training. I had a few weeks of security police training in Texas, and then I was sent to train with the Army on Air Base Ground Defense (ABGD), which is just what it sounds like: a training class on how to defend an Air Force base using Army techniques.

The Army taught us the basics of digging foxholes and field stripping (cleaning) our weapons, land navigation with a compass, and all of those things that a good solider needs to do. But as officers, we would not be judged on the depth of our foxhole or how clean our weapon was. We would be judged on how well we led our soldiers in the field. We would be judged on *their* foxholes, *their* weapons, and *their* ability to deter threats and defend the base. The leader is only as good as their team.

Because the Army knows that in a security police flight or in an infantry squad, the soldiers—the troops—are the ones who get the real work done, our class of officers was merged with classes of young security police soldiers, the kinds of soldiers we would be leading in our units once they completed their training and got deployed.

We were each assigned a squad of about ten young soldiers and given a mission of defeating "enemy" incursions, in a field exercise that would last for several days. And inherent in that mission was the need to take care of those soldiers. In the Army, our instructors made it clear that "troops eat first." It wasn't just a rule to follow or a motto, it was a mindset, a focus, a responsibility. I have also heard it as "leaders eat last," and there is a leadership book by that name. But, in my mind that places the focus on the leaders and the focus needs to be on the troops.

When the chow truck came every morning, bringing warm eggs and lukewarm coffee, we made sure that our troops' needs were taken care of first, pulling half out of the foxholes, while the others continued to watch for the enemy, and then switching. Only after the troops were fed and back in the holes and any instructions were given did the officers pick through what was left and have some of the now-barely-warm coffee. It wasn't good hot, and it was terrible cold.

After training, I kept the "troops eat first" mindset when working with my troops at each of my bases. I made sure the teams had what they needed to be successful. I coached my troops: Don't complain to me about the rain, there's nothing I can do about that. Tell me instead if your rain gear isn't working or has a hole in it; I can get you the proper gear.

In the civilian world, your team are "your troops." They are doing the hands-on coding or answering the phones or doing front-line sales or whatever work your team is responsible for. Without them the job simply won't get done. "Troops eat first" in the civilian world means the leader's job is to always take care of the team before anything else.

That can manifest in many ways. That can be tangible things like making sure "the troops" get upgraded computers if they need to do some work that the standard-issue computers can't handle.

Sometimes "troops eat first" can be as simple as making sure that the team has access to snacks or meals or coffee. In many of my jobs as a consultant, we were given a war room or set of spaces to work in at a client site. In one location, the client had no amenities because they'd been facing budget cuts for years. There was no coffee maker, no vending machine, nothing, and the cafeteria was a ten-minute walk from our assigned cube area. In order to keep team morale up, we ordered a big percolator of coffee from the cafeteria to be brought every morning. We also had a snack center with chocolate, granola bars, chips, etc. The cost to the job was minimal compared to the morale victory. Our clients were invited to partake as well, of course, which also provided a "water cooler" forum for chatting each morning.

Troops eat first can also be intangible support, like managing the upper leadership to make sure timelines aren't too tight, limiting the number of meetings, or clarifying directions from stakeholders, etc.

In Project Falcon, "troops eat first" manifested in a few key ways:

**Getting the right resources.** (*Resource*, or *Human Resource*, are common terms for "people" in the business world). Even though we had made a few key changes in people and roles, there were still a lot of gaps and skills challenges in the team. And one of the pieces of software was less common, and frankly outdated, so there were not a lot of people skilled on it. I set up time and met daily for weeks with the leaders in our company who owned those resource pools to identify the right people to bring onto the team. In a non-consulting context, it would just mean focusing on hiring or contracting the right resources if there are gaps in the team and open job requests to fill.

**Problem solving.** I was never an expert in any of the technologies that my team was working on. I was there to guide and support the team, not solve the complex technology problems myself. But I would always try to learn as much as I could about the technology, so that I could make the right decisions or advise my client where needed. Whenever there was an issue, I would ask as many questions as I could, both to learn about the new technology, but also to force the team to think through the problems we were solving. I was always happy to ask the "dumb" questions that would get the team to find the right answer.

One of the systems was an older technology that was inflexible and challenging to work on. The team came to me one day when they wanted to raise a ticket to the software vendor and said they couldn't solve a problem in the code until the software package was fixed. Getting software vendors to fix anything is never fast, even if they agree to make the change, which is rare.

I asked my team to explain the problem to me. In a nutshell, they needed to pass data to another system, but the software field the data should go in wasn't big enough for all the data we wanted to put in it. I asked, "Could you use a different field? Or could we use two of the fields and put half of the argument in each?" I didn't know if it was possible, but I wanted to get the team thinking and get them unstuck. I could see my questions were making them think differently, and maybe even giving them a glimmer of an idea. The team went back to the drawing board and they had it solved by the end of the day. They ended up using multiple fields, essentially.

In Project Falcon, "troops eat first" meant I did everything I could to make the team and the project successful. Sometimes, they would tell me what they needed, and I could act on it. Other times, the team didn't realize they needed anything; they were just chopping at trees in their forest. In those cases, it would be up to me to see the conflicts and either redirect, re-route, or clear the roadblock.

## TWO-DIMENSIONAL LEADERSHIP

After getting the right resources, supporting the team in the "troops eat first" manner solved the next layer of leadership. The team was starting to move toward the objectives.

But the team wasn't where I wanted it to be yet. It was now focused on doing the right things, but the level of engagement wasn't where I wanted it to be. They were no longer in a pit of misery, but they also hadn't gelled as a team, and people still weren't energized and happy. The team just wasn't where I knew it could be.

I realized that leadership must cover two dimensions to be truly successful. The first of those two dimensions is the "what," for instance, *What is the objective; what are the goals for the team to achieve?*

The second dimension that leadership must cover is the "how." *How is the team to behave and to operate during the achievement of those goals?* Too often, leaders only focus on WHAT needs to get done without focusing on HOW the team should operate while achieving the goal.

## the WHAT

What a team needs to achieve needs to be clear to everyone on the team. There should be overall team goals and individual goals for each team member that contribute to the whole. The team should be measured by their achievement toward those goals at the end of the rating period. It's so obvious and logical that it sounds too easy. How do leaders get this wrong?

I'll provide one clear example of how the WHAT goes wrong, and then I'll provide additional examples in upcoming chapters.

## competing objectives

I worked at several clients where sub-organizations had goals that were competing. A common example is having conflicts between the IT team and the security team or other support teams.

At one company, the IT team's overall objective was to deliver on some major programs, leveraging my company as the development team to get the work done. We had an overall contract, which essentially said for each small project we had to individually contract the project, following the rules of the master contract. Each project would have to pass through security reviews to make sure that anything that we built wouldn't disrupt the current technical ecosystem. We also had to work with the infrastructure and network teams.

On the face of it, there was no problem. Each of those functions—legal, security, network, and development must work together to get the project completed in a safe, compliant way that meet business objectives. The problem in this company was the fact that the legal, security, and infrastructure teams all reported to one boss, and the development team reported to another boss.

On the development side, personnel would be rated and measured by on-time deliveries of the projects. The development boss was only measured on speed of delivery. His team wasn't incentivized to care about security or network stability.

The other boss's team were measured on zero vulnerability for security, zero impact to the network, and the legal team by making sure that they had zero percent liability. The "support structure" boss was only measured on zero defects and liability.

The result is that those two teams were perpetually in conflict.

As a development team, navigating every one of these normally healthy checkpoints felt like armed combat. They should have had a single common goal that took both needs into account, such as the delivery of secure, and on-time projects into the network, so as to minimize disruption to the current environment and liability to the corporation, should issues arise. If they both had the same objective, they would have needed to create some joint policies for security and development, to standardize how best to maximize development in a secure manner.

To use a house-building example, it was as if in this company the general contractor (like the development boss) didn't care about anything but building the house; he wasn't worried about things like getting permits or inspections. If the department responsible for permits and inspections kept changing the rules, or making them up as they went along, or holding the builders up to impossible standards, or if the general contractor didn't design according to the codes and just built whatever they felt would make the timelines—you might have a house built, but you might never be able to move into it. Having the general contractor responsible for the permit and the completion of the inspection makes sure that everything gets coordinated and works together.

This may sound like an extreme example, but I encountered several different companies that had similar challenges, especially with a conflict between security and infrastructure or development, though not to the same extent.

On Project Falcon, the WHAT of the project was clear, although it was very complex. We were to fix the performance of one system that was extremely sluggish, and we had to combine two organizations' systems into one, while continuing to deliver features to the business on both, and without interrupting their work. It was a lot, but with the right team, and with the right support, it was possible.

## the HOW

Once the WHAT has been defined and understood, there is the HOW.

If the WHAT can be measured quantitatively, the HOW is more subjective.

The HOW is more about the culture and the team, and the environment that you want to create while you're working toward the WHAT.

It would have been very easy for every one of my projects to be a "death march" (a common term in IT and consulting circles, which means an unending slog of work, including nights and weekends, to complete a project at all costs) because they were already in crisis when I arrived. But because I believe the best teams deliver the best results, my goal was always to uplift and fix the team so they could be successful. In military terms, I could either win the battle and get the work done in a death march, or I could build a high performing team that not only completed the objectives but went on to serve the client for the duration, winning the war.

On Project Falcon, the team had already been in "death march" mode when I arrived; they were working nights and weekends and were not getting anywhere. They were already miserable; the team spirit was crushed. I couldn't have pushed them any harder. If I had, they would have just started dropping. I needed to rebuild the team and get it working like a strong unit.

After the personnel changes were made and we started making progress, I noticed several problems with the team culture. I started taking notes on the things that needed to change and making corrections.

There was a lot of blame-casting and finger-pointing that needed to stop. People were under such pressure that they would just do what they were told, without really thinking through whether there was a better way. We had some highly skilled technical experts and architects, but they were just updating the system as asked, rather than stepping back, looking at the full solution, and proposing the right way to do things.

Once I'd identified several cultural issues, I established some Project Falcon Guiding Principles based on everything I'd seen going wrong. And then, I set up an All Hands Meeting and walked the team through the principles I wanted them to follow.

Feel free to roll your eyes now; I don't blame you. I have been in multiple organizations where guiding principles had been established and they were lovely words on a wall that meant nothing and were never followed. Writing them and not following them is probably worse than not having any guiding principles. But I felt like the culture needed an overhaul and I needed to tell the team what I wanted to see.

The Project Falcon Guiding Principles I provided to my team in the All Hands Meeting were:
- No Blame, Just Solutions
- One Team
- Communicate
- Give Credit Where Credit Is Due
- Critical Thinking

After establishing my Guiding Principles, I reinforced them in every monthly All Hands Meeting. More importantly, I had to live them myself. If I didn't model them myself, they would never have worked, regardless of how many meetings I proclaimed them in.

Here's one example that put a few of the Principles in practice: There was another company building a system that had to interface with the two that we were responsible for. That other company and that system was being led by a different organization at the client. That is a recipe for disaster if Organization A and Organization B aren't in lockstep on their plans.

Not surprisingly, they were far from being in lockstep. Organization A had us design our system based on the needs of the sales agents who would be using it. Organization B had their system designed based on the needs of the accounting systems that would process orders. When we tried to have data flow from our systems to theirs, we found out there was a major disconnect in terms of how each system was designed.

To keep using the house building example, it was as if a wife had hired ACME Contracting to redesign the kitchen, and the husband had hired Joe's Contracting to redo the bathrooms. ACME Contracting had built the kitchen and assumed where the pipes, electricity, and the gas lines would run, but they hadn't matched their plans to where the plumbing or electric was built for the bathrooms.

On Project Falcon, both managers of their respective organizations tried to blame each other, and they tried to blame each of the respective consulting teams, including me and my team. They expected that we should have known and planned based on what the other system was going to do. Neither consulting team wanted to have to change their system around, and it wasn't a situation in which we could meet in the middle. One of the systems had to change dramatically so that the two systems could connect.

The No Blame, Just Solutions principle applied here, because blame wasn't going to solve anything. I stepped back with my team and asked them to think through the best architectural solution, setting aside any questions of who had to do the work and who was at fault. I asked them the most logical way for the data to be designed, and the most common way in the industry for these types of systems to connect. I told them not to worry about who had to do the work or how much that would cost anyone, but to focus on the right solution.

Re-framing the question to focus on the best solution architecturally led the team to the right questions and the right discussions across the organizations. Once we all agreed on the right solution, we could work with the client separately regarding whether there were any contractual or payment obligations.

If I had yelled at the team for getting the solution wrong, or if I had told them to try to get the other team to do the fix, all of my focus on HOW we wanted to work as a team would have failed. They would have known that although I said, "No blame," I still blamed them.

Also, getting them to use the Critical Thinking principle leveraged their architectural expertise and led to a better solution. If I hadn't addressed that situation according to my own Guiding Principles, they would have been seen as a joke and ignored.

In December that year, I gave all of my team members a small holiday gift—a stress toy for their desks, along with a laminated card printed with my Guiding Principles.

When I went to India to visit my team members there, I brought the same gifts—stress toys and Guiding Principles cards.

Many of my team members took to carrying the Guiding Principles cards in their wallets. I never expected that, but the Guiding Principles took a life of their own, and as my team members adopted them the team dynamic changed.

There were also occasions when I would slip, and I would have a team member say, "Oh, that's not in line with One Team, or Give Credit Where Credit Is Due," and I would have to retract and fix what I had said. They were right to call me out on it.

We went from being a blame-centric team to being solution-oriented. The team stopped simply doing what they were told and put more creative energy into uncovering solutions. The team pulled together, and we finally started gelling as a team.

I also held a contest to add a few more Guiding Principles to the list so that the team could "own" them even more. I'd wanted to make an even list of ten principles, but we ended up with twelve.

Some of the Guiding Principles the team added included:
- Be Proactive
- Make It Work
- Have Fun

I used Guiding Principles with every team after that. There was a core set of five or six that I applied on every project because they always seemed relevant. The last ones I would tailor to meet the specific needs of the project situation.

I'll cover several of these Principles in more detail in upcoming chapters, because most of these I consider to be the absolute baseline for creating a healthy team environment.

## the death march

While I firmly believe that the only way I could have fixed Project Falcon was by fixing the team, and focusing on how the team operated in addition to what we were doing, not all leaders work that way. Where I knew pushing the team harder would break them, some leaders keep pushing teams even when they are in death march mode, and then can't understand why there are issues. Project Triad, one of my last projects, was in "death march" mode, as Project Falcon had initially been, when I was brought in to fix it.

Project Triad was one of the most complex projects I'd ever encountered. The goal was to build four global systems for a company that had been very decentralized and didn't have any global systems. Just building four systems at the same time would have been a huge effort because they were essentially trying to reinvent the way the company does business, across the majority of their processes, from the start of an order to shipping the product to the customer.

The complexity of that alone would have had me advising the customer to re-think their strategy. Most companies will start off by creating one global system and then build additional systems connected to it later. It's like remodeling your entire house while still living in it, instead of starting with the kitchen or a bathroom.

To make it worse, this client had decided to have three different (Competing!) companies doing the work. My company would be responsible for the up-front strategy and design, and then the technical build work would be done by two different companies.

Again, to use the house analogy, it would be like hiring ACME Contractors to design a kitchen and bath remodel project, then giving the design to Joe's Contracting, who would perform the build on the kitchen. Then, have a third company, XYZ Contracting, remodel the bathrooms based on ACME's design. Finally, all of this would be done at the same time, while the house is still occupied by its residents. It is bound to be a confusing mess.

My company was also supposed to be "in charge" of orchestrating and managing the whole program. When I got pulled in, it had been running for seven months, and it had not been going well.

I told my boss, Jimmy, that we needed to restructure the program, but he said there was no way. He said he had done a project like this before so we should be able to make it work. Jimmy wasn't willing to push back and work with the client to rethink and reset the project because he'd already told the client that we could do it. He wasn't willing to look bad in front of the client even though I believed the structural problems would never allow the program to be successful.

I was already the third or fourth leader to step in.

The team was at a breaking point, having worked eighteen hours a day for months. Every Friday Jimmy asked me, "Are they working the weekend?" because all he cared about was getting the deliverables done. ("Deliverables" is a common term that means anything that has to be completed, such as documentation, code designs, or code). But the team was working at about half-power because everyone was so exhausted and felt so beaten down.

I knew the "death march" mode wasn't going to work, and so I started repairing the cracks and rebuilding the team.

Jimmy felt that my team-oriented approach was going to take too long, so I was rolled off.

Jimmy brought in another set of leaders to replace me, three different leaders he believed would be able to drive the team forward. These would be the fifth, sixth, and seventh leaders to try. But the project had run too far aground already. The team was too exhausted, and no amount of yelling and making them work weekends was going to change it.

Not long after I left, Project Triad was canceled, and the team was rolled off. It was never going to work the way it was set up, regardless of how many new leaders were brought in to fix it.

The company then worked with the client to reset, restructure, and restart.

The lesson from this?

You can't win any fights without your team. Pushing your team mercilessly to achieve the WHAT may win a battle, but it won't work over the long term. You have to care about HOW the work is getting done and HOW your team is operating, or eventually, all work will stop. Setting up a structure where the team can thrive is critical for a long-term win.

Project Triad will serve as a counterpoint throughout the rest of the book because there were so many things wrong with it, and the appropriate steps weren't taken to set it up for success.

## THE THIRD DIMENSION

Beyond the WHAT and the HOW, there is a third dimension of leadership, which I'll call the WHEN.

Even though it should be obvious to everyone that the objective needs to be set *before* the team starts working, this doesn't always happen. The problem is that when you're in a pressure-filled situation, or if you don't know the answers, sometimes it's hard to pull back and set the right course before pushing the team forward.

There is a belief that making progress, getting the team to work and getting things done will be helpful, even if the end state hasn't been determined, but it's often not true. Here are some examples of where the objectives were not clarified at the beginning, which resulted in the project going very wrong, and where pausing up front to gain alignment in a similar project resulted in a better outcome.

### where it went wrong

Two companies merged and my company was brought in to enable Company B to operate in Company A's systems. The new goal for "MergeCo," as we'll call them, was for us to create a "technical solution," by which the executives meant for us to just put the right fields and details into the system to accommodate Company B. Unfortunately, MergeCo didn't want to take the time to really understand how both companies operate or align or streamline their processes.

The challenge to merging two companies arises if the companies operate in a very different manner, with different customers, different territories, different policies surrounding who can see orders in progress, and differences regarding the process of reviews or approvals, margin thresholds, sales credit, etc. If none of the processes are harmonized prior to merging, you end up essentially building two entirely different systems in one, and things get messy fast.

Inevitably, things will take longer than they should and there will be more errors than there should be, all because people were too "busy" to do the right things up front. The end result will be more effort and money spent on systems. And worse, if the whole goal of buying Company B in the first place was to have some synergies, or for the companies to align their merged processes, now each of the different processes are built into the systems. Now, if the companies ever want to have synergies, those systems will then need to be updated, too.

It's like if we were told to just technically merge a machine that makes chocolate bars and a machine that makes jellybeans. If there wasn't time up front to figure out if there were common things that had to be done to support both ... and how that could be done ... you'd essentially end up with two machines tied together but creating parallel processes, one part spitting out chocolate bars, and one spitting out jellybeans. Instead of streamlining anything, you've just made your machines more cumbersome.

I was brought in as a reviewer to that project, after the teams started running into delays. At that point, the project had already been running for over a year, so we pushed ahead and got the project done, versus starting over. But it would have been better if they'd gotten some basic alignment on sales processes before we were asked to start building a "technical solution," which really made everything more complicated.

## where it went . . . better

In Project Falcon, a client who asked us to merge two systems which had been operated by two different organizations, had said almost the same thing, "Just do a technical solution." Their meaning was clear: *I don't want to know the details and don't want to spend the time or money to harmonize the processes. I just want to be down to one system so I can reduce my software license costs.* We knew it would not work the way the client wanted, but we also knew that the client didn't want to take the three to six months it would take to standardize the processes.

In this case, we found a middle ground. We provided a list of key processes that needed to be figured out up front so that we wouldn't have to duplicate major functions in the system. They agreed to make decisions on those key processes. This forced the client to develop an understanding of the processes between the two organizations, to make some crucial decisions about how they could work together, and to decide which processes they would follow. The effort caused a "delay" of a few weeks, but it enabled the project to run smoothly and remain on timelines after that.

It's like the old adage, "measure twice, cut once." But when executives say something like "Just do a technical solution," it's more like saying: "Just have the carpenter figure it out." If the blueprint hasn't been defined, the carpenter can measure all day long before cutting a board, and he or she will still end up with a bunch of useless lumber, cut without a plan, blueprint, or vision.

It would have been better if they had standardized *all* of their processes first, but at least standardizing the key ones kept us from duplicating the whole system, and it kept the project on track.

## YOU CAN'T FIX IT ALONE

After getting the right team, giving them strong support, and then resetting the culture on Project Falcon, there were still challenges.

The last element I had to deal with had nothing to do with the team itself. In fact, I had been so focused on the team, on what we needed to do to clean our own house, that I hadn't realized how some of the problems within the broader company were affecting us.

As I'd mentioned before, consulting is setting up a team within the broader client team. If there are challenges with the client team, or with the interaction between the client team and the consulting team, the project can run into troubles. In this case, getting the key clients on board to help was the final piece of the puzzle.

I had two primary clients, the IT owner and the business owner. They were at odds, which always makes a project more difficult. I had resolved from the beginning to treat them both equally and fairly and to be transparent with both.

In particular, the business owner was extremely challenging to work for. He was very demanding and very perceptive. He'd called us out multiple times when things were going wrong. Since it was a recovery, during the first couple of months everything was still going wrong, and he was absolutely right to call us out.

I had set up a weekly one-on-one with him, and I always had a list of topics that I planned to cover, like what was going well and what I was trying to fix. I wanted him to walk away from those meetings feeling reassured that things were on track, or at least getting better.

After several months we'd had a particularly bad week, and everything seemed bleak. Not only had I not put a list together for our discussion, I didn't have the heart to think about it. I walked into his office with a blank page in my notebook. I said, "Hello," and asked, "How are you?"

He said, "No list?"

I said, "No, no list."

Instead, this time I listened. And it changed the entire relationship. He told me what he thought was going wrong, and we had a dialogue about the ways things could be fixed. He knew some of the challenges in his own organization and how they affected us, and the truth of the matter was that we could solve them better together.

I won't say that after that he was no longer demanding or that he stopped calling me out; he was, and he did so multiple times. But we listened to each other, we worked together, and we eventually got the whole program turned around.

Working with him made me realize I'd had a blind spot. Being focused on the team is right and necessary but it is likely not sufficient. My experience in the military, leading a team of troops that was very isolated from the rest of the workings of the base, had allowed me to focus on the troops and not worry as much about the larger organization. But on Project Falcon that approach became a problem.

The business owner taught me one of the biggest lessons I learned on Project Falcon. I had been so committed to telling my stakeholders all of the improvements we were making and giving them peace about all of our progress, that I'd failed to bring them on board and get them invested in helping us solve the problems.

Getting them on board made a world of difference.

When I eventually left Project Falcon to go to my next big program, the business owner asked if there was anything he could do for me. He offered to write me a letter of recommendation, which no one had ever offered before. It wasn't necessary; we didn't use that sort of thing in the company, but I took him up on it because he'd offered. And it was the nicest letter anyone had ever written for me.

Later in the book, I'll focus more on leading within large organizations, as well as managing your career, both of which require you to manage and build relationships with your key stakeholders and bosses.

## STRONG TEAMS: SUMMARY

The culmination of our efforts on Project Falcon was a weekend release. (A "release" is when code that has been developed is put onto the production systems. "Production systems" are the ones that real-life users like call center agents use, versus copies of the systems that are used for testing.) The goal of the release was to merge the two systems into one.

For the release, not only did we need to update one system to include all of the features of the second, but we had to transfer the data from one system to the other. There was a lot of data to transfer, and working with data can be very challenging and time consuming.

We chose to do the release on Labor Day weekend, so that we could have the systems down for three days and not impact the workforce who used those systems. We had conference rooms reserved in the client company for everyone in the US to work in, and the whole team was prepared to be on site the whole time. I also sent one of my leaders to India to more tightly connect our team there with our US teams during the release weekend.

We all arrived at the client building on Saturday morning of Labor Day weekend, after having worked all week to get ready for the deployment. We faced a minor hitch when the badge of one of our team members wouldn't work, having expired — it was September 1$^{st}$—and I had to call a friend who was an executive assistant at the company to grant him access.

And then it was on. We had scripted the deployments, and we had a deployment plan, and we followed it. My job was making sure we stayed on track, making sure communications went out according to plan to keep the clients informed of our progress, and making sure food and drinks came in to keep the troops watered.

At one point, I looked around at midnight and realized that all of my leaders were awake, in both India and in the US, and that we would run aground if I didn't start getting people rest. I sent two back to the nearby hotel to sleep and made sure the junior members of the team were similarly rotating so that we wouldn't all burn out.

I slept for two hours on a bench on the side of the conference room.

Of course, there were issues, but we jumped on the phone with the software companies to get the issues resolved, or we called the clients to join the conference calls when we needed them.

The deployment was ultimately extremely successful, and it was deemed by the client as one of their most successful to date.

The team was elated; we had not only accomplished the WHAT of merging the systems, but we had also worked according to the HOW as well. Our team was tired, but it was the tired of a team who had done a great job and was satisfied, not "death march" tired.

To me, that release was exactly what I had been striving for with the team. I had wanted to lead the team to accomplish the objectives, but to do so in a way that made the team stronger, that made them proud, and that made them want to tackle the next set of objectives.

To me, that's leadership. The shocking thing is that not everyone understands that or operates the same way.

During the entire three-day weekend, none of the client personnel showed up to support us, or even just to say hello and thank the team. Not one of them. It was only my team who was there.

On Tuesday, I went into the office. I had made it to my hotel to sleep sometime on Monday night, after having slept about two hours the whole weekend. My team wasn't much better off, all still short on sleep.

I said to the client who was supposedly the lead for the effort, "The deployment went well."

"Yes," he said, "you put the right team in place and everything goes well; that's leadership."

I blinked. *Was he joking? Was he taking credit for this?* He wasn't there. He didn't even come by to thank the team. He didn't even join any of the phone calls. I think I mumbled something like, "That's leadership," and walked away.

I knew what it took to get that job over the line. And we had done it in a way that pulled us together. We had finally become the right team. We had completed the objectives of the WHAT, but we had done it in a way that matched the culture I'd wanted to create, the HOW. We had become a strong team and had flown like Project Falcon was supposed to.

After Project Falcon got straightened out, I got branded as a "fixer" and spent most of my ten to twelve years as an executive either fixing teams or leading challenging teams. With each new team that I "fixed," I learned more about the things that could go wrong and how to either repair those issues or avoid them altogether. I became a better fixer and a stronger leader.

I did the "fixing" my way, focusing on the team and not just the outcomes. I would listen to the team, understand the conflicts, and determine where the gaps were and what had gone wrong with the client. I did this by peeling back all of the layers of the issues until we started turning chaos into order and despair into energy.

2.

# ONE OBJECTIVE TO RULE THEM ALL: PROJECT ASCEND CASE STUDY

One of the hardest jobs in my career as a "fixer" was taking over a team working on Project Ascend. Project Ascend had been running for three years, and I was brought in to clean it up based on escalations from the company's president. In those three years, nothing had been deployed to production and the project was severely delayed and over budget.

I found the Project Ascend culture and environment to be horrible, far worse than Project Falcon had been, which I hadn't thought was possible. The clients were literally screaming and yelling at us on calls. I'd never heard that level of animosity and unprofessionalism before.

People on all sides were escalating but not communicating. And everyone was miserable. You could feel the misery in the "war room," where my team worked. It was palpable. There was hate dripping off the walls.

There was so much work to get that project "right." My company was relying on a subsidiary company (SubCo) for a lot of the work, but my company was blaming the SubCo for all of the problems. And of course, the SubCo blamed my company. I had to fix the relationship between my company and SubCo. I also had to fix the relationship with the client, stop the escalations, and, most importantly, get the work done and out the door into production so the company could have a working system.

Project Falcon had been like an onion. Only after I'd fixed the first layer had I seen what the next set of issues were. This project wasn't like that. Project Ascend was more like a puzzle. It was as if someone had kicked and stomped on the pieces, many of which were now scattered, broken, or lost. There were multiple pieces that needed to be worked on, and I felt like I had to tackle them all at once. There were a few hidden pieces that I'd have to find later, but there were so many pieces to deal with at once.

I leveraged lessons learned from Project Falcon and the Guiding Principles I'd developed there. I focused first on "One Team," since the team was so broken, as well as "No Blame, Just Solutions," since blame was the primary source of the friction. There were several other Guiding Principles and lessons I'd have to employ to get through the project, but that's where I had to start.

## ONE TEAM

When I first walked in to fix Project Ascend, I stood in the middle of the "war room" and watched the interactions of the team. I watched the lead I was replacing fire off escalations to the clients who were two floors up, and I watched her reaction when they fired back counter-blame.

There were three companies involved in the work: the software vendor, my consulting company, and the subsidiary company of ours, SubCo. There were also multiple key clients and organizations within the client's company, including the business lead, the IT group, a North American group, and a European group.

My company was blaming SubCo for not getting the work done. SubCo was blaming my company for not setting any boundaries with the client and being too focused on additional sales. The client blamed both my company and SubCo and was pitting us against each other. And the software company was whispering in the clients' ears, telling them that we didn't know what we were doing. It was clear that we weren't going to get anywhere unless we started working as a team, and we couldn't do that if we all kept throwing each other under the bus.

The first thing I focused on was getting my company and SubCo on the same sheet. In order to be a strong team, the team needs to think of itself as a team. A single team. If a team has silos and divisions and there is animosity between groups, the team will not function properly. Unless we could resolve our inner strife, we weren't going to go anywhere.

In order to do that, I started building a relationship with the head of SubCo, Dan. I listened to his perspective of what had gone wrong and what needed to be done to get things moving in the right direction.

Peter, my company's lead on the account, was part of the blame game and kept his finger firmly pointed at SubCo. I told him that he had to step away from the program and that I wouldn't be reporting to him, a bold move in my company because it was his account and he had more seniority than me.

When I told Dan and the other SubCo leaders that I didn't report to Peter and I had sent him away, they knew that I had the power to change things, and they were more open to me. That one move, removing a constant source of blame and division, significantly changed the dynamic between myself and the SubCo leaders.

After I had built a relationship with Dan, I got Dan's agreement to restructure the team so that everyone reported to me, regardless of whether they worked for my company, or the SubCo. I intentionally didn't learn which company everyone worked for. I restructured the team based on role and skill, with everyone rolling up to me. Dan stayed part of the team but didn't make any operational decisions.

Even though I reorganized the team so that everyone reported up to me, I didn't have the same leeway with rolling people on or off as I would have with people solely from my company. Only if I had a major challenge with one of the resources could I work with Dan to get an individual removed, and I only did that once. For the most part, I had to work with the resources that were on the team and shift the team dynamic from frustration and blame to a positive environment.

I spent a lot of time listening to each of the key leaders on the team. I met with the architect, the delivery lead, and the functional leads to understand where they felt like the real challenges were. Taking the time to listen, especially to the technical and functional experts from SubCo, made a huge impact.

The next thing I did was set up recurring, frequent All Hands Meetings, and I made sure that the full team, including both my company and SubCo, were invited. At the first couple of meetings, I provided a rundown of all of the changes we were making and how we were restructuring the contract. The SubCo team members were given equal treatment and were able to raise questions and be answered openly (which had not happened under my predecessor's leadership).

Because the project had been under fire from the client, leadership from both my company and SubCo would stop by occasionally. Whenever leadership from one company came, I made sure that team members from both companies were included in the All Hands or happy hours with leadership.

Leadership from both sides at first protested that, wanting to meet with just their side of the team, but I held firm. I told them, "We are one team; you meet with the whole team, or you don't come."

Gradually, the team, especially the SubCo team members, saw that I wasn't going to "say" I was going to treat them equally but not follow through. They had been treated like second class citizens by my predecessors and so they were right to be on guard. But they saw that everyone was going to be treated equally, based on role and the needs of the team, not based on which badge they wore.

I also made efforts to understand SubCo, which has different levels, different leadership, and different rules than my company. My predecessor had gotten frustrated that the SubCo team members and leadership wouldn't follow some of my company's policies. However, even though it is a subsidiary, it is legally a different company and has different policies; the SubCo leadership was correct to follow its own company policies.

Gradually, the lines blurred, and we became a real team. The team started to work better together, and the client stopped trying to pit us against each other. It took months to get to that point. It took several more months until we really gelled and trusted each other.

Fixing a project by strengthening the team, while also fixing the structural problems, may not be the fastest way to do things. But I still believe it's the only way to do them. I don't think we would ever have been able to deliver on Project Ascend if we hadn't fixed the divisions within the team.

## project triad: the counterpoint

While the example of Project Ascend was very obvious because of the division between my company and SubCo, I have seen as stark a division between members of my own company who were from different units.

When I was tasked with fixing Project Triad, beyond the structural problems I mentioned earlier (building four systems with three competing companies), the Triad team had a rift a mile wide between the technical people and the strategic people in my own company. The leaders of each area could hardly be in the same room before arguing, even in front of their teams.

The first thing I did was try to understand the nature of the rift and figure out how to get each side to understand the others' point of view so that we could work together better.

The strategy team was comprised primarily of MBA grads, who are used to working with executives and mapping out strategies. The tools of their trade are PowerPoint, visioning sessions, workshops, and strategic blueprints. They had knocked the socks off the client through their initial visioning sessions which had drawn out the long-range vision for the company's end to end global systems.

The technology team was comprised of people who had tons of experience in designing systems for use in various functional areas, including finance, supply chain, and product engineering, but speak and think more technically, and aren't skilled at vision sessions and workshops.

The problem was the client had gotten used to the strategy team's style and wanted the technology team to operate the same way. But they didn't. The technology team felt like they were trying to live up to a standard that didn't make sense for the work they needed to do. They also felt like the strategy team had outlined an amazing vision but hadn't gathered enough details from the vision sessions to be useful for the technical design. So the technology team felt like they had to essentially start from scratch.

It was as if the strategy team had painted a beautiful picture of a modern house on a mountain with big windows, the sun shining through the clouds, and the client wanted that house! But in order to design and it, the technology team needed to understand things like, how big the house should be, how many bathrooms it should have, and whether it should be open concept or have a separate kitchen and dining room. The strategy team felt like the technology team was just poorly organized and not that competent. It was bad.

I started to build relationships with both the strategic and technical sides, and to help each understand the other's point of view. It was like translating between Greek and Martian they were so far apart.

The rift was not only at the leadership level, but it also permeated the lower levels. I would join meetings with the junior leaders, and if it was a meeting set up by the tech team I'd ask where their strategy counterparts were. The same applied if it was a meeting set up by strategy leaders. There were status meetings just for strategy people and others for just tech. I started ripping down those walls and merging meetings so that we could all meet together as a team before going to the client with ideas or solutions.

I started seeing changes, and the rift started to improve, but the ship turned too slowly for my boss and for the client. They were expecting some sort of jackrabbit fix which got everything fixed quickly. That's when I was rolled off the project and new leadership was brought in.

I heard later that the effect of my focus on improving the team dynamics had made a lasting change on the team and the team was able to work together better through the end of the design phase, when the majority of the team was rolled off.

One other element of "One Team," or lack thereof, I saw on multiple teams was the lack of diversity, or where there wasn't equal treatment. If you want a strong team, One Team, you will also need to focus on supporting all of your players, regardless of their background.

## LEVEL THE PLAYING FIELD

On Project Ascend, there was a wide range of diversity in our war room. We had people from South Africa, New Zealand, and the Netherlands. We had men, women, several veterans, and all ages, from recent college grads to people on the cusp of retirement.

Just as my focus was on making sure that everyone on my team was treated fairly and as a single team, whether they were from my company or from SubCo, I was also interested in making sure men, women, and every other diverse experience had a fair shot to demonstrate their capabilities.

Supporting women in their career growth has always been particularly important to me, as I'd been fighting that battle my whole career, starting in the military. So, when I saw examples of women not having the same opportunities on Project Ascend, I knew I had to step in.

My first experience with a women's leadership effort came at the Air Force Academy when I was a freshman cadet. I was part of the graduating class of 1991. Women had been allowed into the Academy with the graduating class of 1980, so 1979 was unofficially known as LCWB, the Last Class with Balls. At the time, 1991 seemed a lifetime away from 1980, so it seemed like women at the Academy were well-entrenched and that the way had been paved before us. But we were only the eleventh class to graduate with women, and admittance did not equate to "acceptance" or equal-footing.

There were about 20 percent women in the Cadet Wing, which in practical terms meant that for each flight or unit of twenty to twenty-five cadets, four to five of them would be women.

During basic training, the men would get buzz cuts, just like you see on the movies. The women got super short cuts that looked like they were done with knives to make them the least attractive as possible, but we still had hair. Which meant that the four to five of us women would stand out and be immediately recognizable amongst the twenty men who all had shaved heads and were nearly indistinguishable.

We couldn't blend into the crowd, and any error made by any of us stood out that much more. The upper-class cadre, our trainers, learned our names faster and they watched us closer. If one of us messed up, it was "women" screwing up, and there was a subtext questioning whether we could handle it, and whether they should've let us in. If a man messed up, it was just a man messing up.

Major Johnson was a female officer who volunteered to meet with the women in our squadron about leadership. I don't think I'd ever even seen a female officer yet, so I was very excited to meet her. I thought she would teach us the ways that she had learned to apply leadership as a woman and how it could help us in our careers.

Major Johnson met with about ten of us female cadets in a back room. She wore a skirt with heavy "low quarter" shoes, black leather men's shoes that had been shrunk to fit women but were in no way feminine or made for women. After doing a quick introduction, she started: "If you choose to wear make-up, you should keep it as neutral as possible, so as not to call attention to yourself."

She spoke half of the time about grooming standards, and the other half of the time about the harassment she'd faced in the military. "Close your legs, I can smell you all the way over here," someone had said to her.

I couldn't believe what I was hearing. Was this really what she wanted to tell us about? Was this the most important thing for us? Not what it was like to be in charge of men and how best to work with men? But how to blend in, and the kinds of abuse we'd be exposed to? In my time at the Academy, I never had another women's mentoring or leadership session, which is just as well if it was going to be as disconcerting and damaging as the first.

Within my first week of arriving at my first duty station in Grand Forks Air Force Base (AFB), North Dakota, I got pulled into what was called a "father-daughter" talk. I was the only female lieutenant (LT) in the security police unit, and the captain pulled me into his office and shut the door. I wore no makeup (despite her horrible training session, I still took Major Johnson's advice), and I had pulled my hair back in a tight braid, per regulations, but I was still obviously female and stood out from my male colleagues.

My father-daughter talk consisted of two main points. First, the captain told me not to date the troops, which I never would have. Fraternization between officers (which I was) and enlisted personnel (aka "the troops") was drilled into us from the first day we walked into the Academy. It was a barrier I would never have crossed.

The second point was even more frustrating. He asked if I was strong enough to carry my weapon. As a security police officer in Grand Forks, ND, my mission was to guard our country's nuclear weapons, and I would be carrying an M-16 semi-automatic rifle with 240 rounds of ammunition. *Was I strong enough? Was he serious?* I had been through four years of the Academy, including obstacle courses, survival class, water survival, and jumping out of airplanes . . . in addition to being an intercollegiate gymnast. I might've been smaller than the guys, but I was strong. *Was he serious, could I carry a weapon?*

The father-daughter chat was repeated at my next duty station, with the same two essential elements being discussed, and I was monitored to determine my ability to do my job. The men I served with were all assumed to be competent until they proved otherwise. As a woman, I had to first prove myself to be competent.

After my father-daughter chat in Grand Forks, I was sent out to the missile field to train with one of the senior lieutenants I would be replacing, LT Smith, who was moving onto his next assignment. He explained the rules of the road while we drove around the missile field and checked on the flight of troops serving in that part of the field.

LT Smith made a few radio calls back to base, using his designated call sign, Roger 7, which indicated that he was the officer in charge of Flight 7. He did it a few times, and he then passed me the mic and said, "You try it."

I said, "Base Control, this is Roger 7," and waited for their response. Nothing happened. I tried two more times and was met with silence.

He took the mic back and they responded immediately, "Go ahead, Roger 7." We tried a few more times that tour of duty, but Base Control would never respond to me.

Once the tour was over and we returned to base, LT Smith and I walked to the command center. He asked, "What happened; why didn't you respond to Roger 7?"

They said, with no shame or embarrassment, "There aren't any female lieutenants so we thought it was a prank." I was standing right there. My shiny new second lieutenant bars were on my uniform. I was a female LT and not a prank.

While they didn't apologize to me, from that day forward, they answered my radio calls when I spoke . . . but it wasn't just assumed, and none of the men had to go through anything like that. They just did their job and were responded to. I had been humiliated first.

When I left the military and joined my consulting firm, I had no idea what the civilian world was, much less corporate consulting. I immediately felt that the civilian world, and my company in particular, was very supportive of women. It felt freeing and comfortable not to have the discrimination I'd felt in the military.

But at some point, I realized that my whole leadership structure was filled primarily by men, with only a few women in key leadership positions. I started to see that there was still discrimination, it was just less overt. It was hidden in unconscious biases and insidious structures. In the military it had almost been easier to deal with because it was in your face. At least you knew when you were being discriminated against.

I joined women's mentoring groups to learn how to overcome this hidden discrimination. I also led women's mentoring groups and mentored women on the teams that I was leading. In all of the groups I joined or led, I learned that there is a long list of things that women can do better to advance in a world where they are measured against men, and where the decision-makers are largely still men.

Here are a few examples: Women are culturally less comfortable with marketing the work they've done than their male counterparts. Women tend to do less networking and relationship-building, which is critical to career advancement. Women tend to use the word "we," whereas a man is more prone to use "I," regardless of what their actual contribution was. Which we all know, but which, despite that fact, people still subconsciously think a man did more because he said "I."

Everything I learned in all of those women's mentoring and women's leadership classes seemed to be focused on making women the best versions of themselves, addressing these traits that seem to hold us back. But none of the mentoring made a material difference, because nothing addressed the underlying issues. Even if women become the best versions of themselves and embody all of the lessons being taught in those women's mentoring classes, the playing field is not level. There are structural and unconscious biases that make the road more difficult for women. We have to level the playing field if we're going to make a real difference.

As Leaders, it's critical for the health of our teams to make sure that we're leveraging all of the talents of our team members and giving all of our team members an equal opportunity to succeed. We all have unconscious biases, but we need to be aware of what they are and guard against them.

Here are just a couple of common examples of unconscious biases and structural challenges, which came up during Project Ascend:

## women are assumed not to want leadership roles

During a planning session for the next phase of work on Project Ascend, we were whiteboarding the team structure. One of the leaders on my team, who would absolutely identify as someone in support of diversity, said, "Jennifer would be great for this role, but she doesn't want a leadership position."

My warning flags went up because I knew Jennifer and she was extremely capable and was already acting as an informal leader by speaking up and mentoring people on the team. I said, "Have you asked her?"

He said, "No, I haven't, but she seems happy doing what she's doing."

I said, "Ask her. Unless she personally says no, we'll assume that's her role."

He asked Jennifer, who said she would be excited to take on that role.

This example was particularly painful because the leader was committed to women, and he was, in his mind, supporting Jennifer by doing what he thought she wanted. He didn't even realize that he was acting on an unconscious bias (Because they're unconscious!) and could have given the position to a man and held Jennifer's career progress back because of it.

## women do more administrative tasks

If there is a woman on a Zoom call or in a meeting, she will most likely be asked to set up the next call or take the notes even if she isn't the most junior person on the team (even if she's the most senior).

Women typically are given the tasks of setting up outings, buying the birthday cakes, or organizing the "fun" activities. The problem with all of these administrative tasks is that if women are having to focus on writing the notes or setting up the next meeting, they aren't free to do the more strategic work. And more problematically, people think that's all the women are capable of.

There were two brand new people on Project Ascend, one man and one woman, both of whom had the same experience, essentially none. One was paired up with the lead for deployment planning, a very technical role that plans all of the steps of getting software out to production during a release. The other new joiner was put in an administrative role, managing a project plan and other tasks as needed. One was female, one was male. Guess which was put in which role, and guess which one would be up for promotion first based on their "contributions."

When I got there and noticed the disparity in the roles for the two people, the young man was doing a good job on the deployment planning, so instead of disrupting his role, I started making sure that the young woman was given additional responsibilities to give her an equal opportunity to prove her capabilities.

The concepts in the section "Level the Playing Field" really apply in two different contexts. As we saw in the Project Ascend examples, you need to make sure everyone on your team is being treated fairly so that they can have the right roles to contribute on the job.

There is also a need to focus on diversity in managing careers, both in terms of managing your own career, as well as in helping others manage theirs. We'll cover more "Level the Playing Field" concepts in the "Manage Your Career" section later in the book.

On Project Ascend, treating everyone fairly, whether men, women, my company, or SubCo, was a critical element to our success. But being One Team and supporting everyone on my team was far from everything I needed to do to get the team working right.

Almost as soon as I walked in the doors at Project Ascend, I realized I had to focus on more than just the team—while the team was very broken, there were tons of challenges in the overall company environment, starting with WHAT we were being asked to do.

## MORE ON THE WHAT...

In my first week at Project Ascend, the CIO asked me to summarize all of the things wrong with the project. While I had started to tackle the One Team problem right away, because it was obvious from the moment I stepped into the room, that first week I documented every other issue I saw and spent the next months working them.

The next several chapters of the book all happened very much in parallel. While I've had to sequence each of them for the book, I was working on all of them at once, trying to find, fix, and fit the puzzle pieces into the board.

As we saw in the last case study, I'd found that on Project Falcon the team itself was the biggest reason the project hadn't been doing well. We had the wrong people in the wrong roles and there had been very little leadership. Most of my fixes were about the team, and HOW the team was operating.

But on Project Ascend, within that first week's investigation, one of the major problems that came to light, and probably the biggest reason that the project had taken three years so far, was that the objectives of the project were not clear. No one knew definitively WHAT we were supposed to deliver.

There were several stakeholders in the project, each of whom wanted something different from it, and none of whom had come to any alignment.

The corporate business team wanted better data so they could better manage the sales and the field workers and report on it to the corporate leadership.

The IT leadership owned the budget, so they wanted to make sure that the project was as cheap as possible and kept using the term MVP, or "minimal viable product." In IT's view MVP meant as few features and capabilities as possible. But they couldn't define the minimum requirements.

The European division didn't want the system in the first place and felt like it was being forced on them by corporate (it was), so they wanted every single feature in their current system that had been lovingly developed and custom-designed to meet their every need for the past twenty years. They were essentially asking us to rebuild their entire custom system into the software package.

The North America division wanted to get off their (very old, very outdated) mainframe system, so they wanted a whole slew of features also, but different ones than Europe's set of features.

Within the first week I realized this, so I met with the business lead. I told him, "One of the biggest problems with Project Ascend is you don't have aligned objectives."

He said, "I don't agree." He added: "I don't know what our objectives are, but we're aligned on them."

What! He wasn't being sarcastic or cute; he was serious. He saw no misalignment but couldn't spell out the objectives if I paid him.

In every meeting, I kept trying to push the point that they needed to all agree on a definition of our objectives. But we weren't making any progress on it because they didn't agree there was a problem in the first place.

Then, my boss and I forced our way into a meeting with all of the presidents, including the division presidents, and I repeated the same challenge. "You're not aligned on your objectives."

"Of course we are," the North American president said. "Our objective is to get off of the mainframes."

"It's not to lose any of the functionality we need," said the European president.

"It's to build the minimal product so it can be as cheap as possible," said the CIO.

There was silence as they finally heard each other.

Essentially, what had been happening for three years was the European and North America divisions were telling us every single feature they wanted. They were like kids in a candy store, while the IT leadership was angry at how much money was being spent. But instead of blaming the regions for all of their demands or controlling them, they blamed us. It's not the job of the clerk in the candy store to tell the kids no when they're buying candy; that's the job of the parents. But the CIO and the corporate leads didn't want to play the parental role and push back on the regions. All of them wanted to blame us.

The only way to progress in the project was to agree on WHAT we had to build so we could build it, get it tested, and get it out the door. To do that, we had to get all of those stakeholders to agree and get them in the same boat together.

## WHERE THERE IS A MORALE PROBLEM, THERE IS A DISCIPLINE PROBLEM

While the CIO and the business lead didn't initially believe they were misaligned on the objectives of the program (I'm still shaking my head in disbelief at that!), they did agree with me that we needed to operate much more tightly with the key stakeholders.

When I pointed out the obvious issue that none of the regional stakeholders were on the weekly Steering Committee Meetings (a senior-level meeting designed to monitor the progress of the project and make relevant decisions where necessary), we restructured the meeting attendees and times to accommodate the regions.

As I started looking at all of the meetings and the mechanisms to manage the project, everything seemed poorly structured and haphazard. In order to address the structural problems of the project, there was one more lesson from the military I needed to leverage.

After two years in North Dakota, I was stationed in Korea at Osan Air Force Base, south of Seoul. Korea is considered a "remote" assignment, which means it's a one-year tour of duty where service members can't bring their families, which can be a hardship, especially for families with kids.

When I first got to Korea and took over, my flight morale was low. In North Dakota, morale was especially a problem for the younger troops, because there aren't a lot of things to do in North Dakota, especially in the winter. But the older troops loved it, because North Dakota is a great place for families with great schools and low crime, and the missile field schedule gave them three days at home. Some of my troops chose to stay for multiple tours and had been there for over ten years. That also led to a lot of knowledge and cohesion on the flight because there were a lot of the same people on the team year over year.

In Korea, on the other hand, since everyone was only on a one-year tour, there was constant turnover of the troops, which meant there was very limited unit cohesion and less knowledge about the specifics of their posts. Additionally, the morale of the older generation who had left their families was low, and the younger troops had a tendency to go off-post after work hours and spend their time at the bars. It was an environment ripe for challenges.

When I took over the flight, Sergeant G was my right-hand man. When I told him I thought the flight had a morale problem, he said, "If there is a morale problem, there is a discipline problem."

It seemed counterintuitive, and I argued with him. I'd been in the military all of two years at that point, versus his ten to fifteen years, but I wasn't quite the newborn babe I'd been on my first assignment either, so I pressed the point. "Being in Korea is hard. People are away from their families; they need support."

"They've had too much coddling already; that's the problem," Sergeant G said.

I listened. He explained that if there is no discipline, people feel they aren't treated evenly. People who are working hard and doing the right things will resent if people who are slacking are treated the same. The hard workers might start slacking in response.

We talked through what we needed to do to bring the discipline back. We needed to be even-handed with everyone, and make sure that everyone was maintaining high standards in terms of uniform, knowledge of their post, and being on time, etc.

We visited the troops regularly when they were on their posts and made them go through their post checks and drills before checking in and chatting. It made a difference, and our team's morale started climbing; you could feel the difference.

Discipline is like the skeleton of an organization. If your bones are strong and sound, you never notice them. If your bones aren't healthy, like if you've broken something or if you have arthritis in your joints, then everything is harder and more painful.

In the civilian world, the principle is the same. Organizations that are lacking in the fundamentals are going to be lacking in morale. You can't just set up a happy hour and turn people's morale around if there are things structurally wrong with the job.

If I had tried to fix Project Ascend, or any of my recovery jobs, by setting up happy hours every Friday, but leaving the underlying problems in place, I would have been thrown out by my client, and the team would have helped. In those recovery jobs, no amount of "happy" hours was going to solve the underlying problems.

I think of "discipline" in the civilian world as the way a team is structured and governed. There are a couple of areas to focus on.

## governance and controls

Governance is the set of meetings and materials by which a project is governed, usually including lower-level detailed meetings, as well as senior-level decision and status meetings, like the Steering Committee. Sounds terribly boring, right? And it probably also seems like these kinds of meetings would be the last thing you'd need to bother with when the whole project seemed to be on fire. Hate and blame, and three years overdue, and I'm worrying about meetings? Really?

Really! Without the right meetings to get people together to make decisions and face up to what's happening, projects can run unchecked or run aground, which is precisely what had happened on Project Ascend. Governance is the "discipline" of a project. If it's running well, it is so seamless that no one notices it, like the bones of a body. But if it's not working well, everything will feel harder.

The first change I made to the governance was getting the regional leadership into the same Steering Committee Meetings with the IT and corporate business leadership. Since the regional divisions, whose disparate objectives were trying to steer the ship in multiple different directions, were providing all of the requirements, we needed everyone in the same meetings to chart the same course. Once we did that, we at least had a single forum to make decisions so that we could start steering the ship in one single direction.

Not surprisingly, the lower-level status meetings were just as dysfunctional, and they also needed to be reset. When I first arrived, the IT leadership wanted a status meeting every day. And every day when the team showed them the status, they wanted a different format, more data, or different graphs. Every day the team leads would spend hours chasing down and calculating the different status and format requests, which kept the team from focusing on what the client really was concerned about, which was making progress.

After a few days of this (I was initially in listen-and-learn mode), I stepped in and said we couldn't focus on the project if we spent all day focused on status gymnastics. We held one meeting to go through the format and get their alignment on it, and then we went forward with that format. Over the next few days, whenever the clients tried to add new things or change the format, I pushed back and said we had to focus on delivering the work. They backed down and we moved forward with the format we'd all agreed on earlier. I don't think anyone from my team had ever pushed back before. Or if they had, the client had never listened before.

Again, it seems simple, but it freed up hours the team needed to focus on the real work, versus chasing their tails on different versions of the data every day.

There were several other basic structural changes I had to make, like setting up a leadership team that included both my company's leadership and that of SubCo. Setting up the frequent All Hands Meetings with everyone to set the direction and keep everyone informed. I also set up one-on-ones with all of the key clients including weekly meetings with the CIO to raise issues and get them resolved.

Getting the baseline structure set up didn't solve all of the problems, of course, but it gave us the mechanisms and the forums for solving the problems. And it got us all in the same ship, which hadn't been the case before.

Below are a few more examples from other projects to clearly illustrate the importance of sound discipline and governance:

## project structure

A chief technology officer (CTO) called my company looking for help with a project. I met with him to understand the challenges and see if we could help.

The CTO told me that there was a major project going on at his company, and it was over budget and months behind. There were several software and consulting companies involved in the project, but not my company. He wanted an outside perspective to provide him with an assessment and a roadmap out of the mess. The "upside" for us, he said, was that we might get to step in and lead or do some of the work.

All of the red flags were waving by this point, and I knew there was little "upside" to getting anywhere near that project. It was clearly a mess, and it was going to be very hard to turn around, especially if there were multiple consulting companies already in the mix.

Then the CTO said he wanted us to do the assessment "from a technology point of view." He was very clearly making a point, like when the professor emphasizes something that is going to be on the test.

I asked, "What do you mean, 'from a technology point of view'?"

In response, he essentially repeated himself but added that he'd want us to look at the design of the systems, the testing practices, and the conversion practices, etc. I'd been around enough goat rodeos to know that what he was saying just didn't match the scene he was painting. It was like asking me to assess the quality of the waitstaff at a failing restaurant without looking at the food being served.

I said, "We can do that . . . but I have to say, very rarely in these kinds of projects is the technology the problem. Usually, it's misaligned objectives where different stakeholders want different things. Or it's poor governance, bad team dynamics, or internal politics. Very rarely is it due to something like testing practices."

We were on video, and the CTO threw his head back and laughed. I was right and he knew he'd been busted. He leveled with me then. "I'm not the sponsor of this program but obviously my people are involved and we're impacted by it. If I bring someone in to do an assessment of the whole program, I'll get crushed by the politics. But if I were to bring in someone to look at the technology, that's in my remit. And

I figured that many of the real problems would get exposed during the technology review."

That phone call is the best example to me of a team not having the basics right. There were internal politics in the company that didn't allow the CTO to do the things he knew needed to be done for the project. All the likely problems I called out were probably in play, like competing objectives, unclear goals, or poor governance. And, more importantly, both the internal company employee teams and the consulting teams were probably miserable. No amount of team happy hours were going to change that. The basic structure of the team was broken. The teams were fighting just to survive.

The only way to improve the program was to get the structure right, improve the overall discipline, and pave a single road forward for the team.

## governance

In another example, a client CFO asked my boss for help with a project being run by one of my peers. My boss asked me to review the project and make recommendations to the CFO.

I met with several leaders from my company to understand the situation from their perspective. I then interviewed a few people from the client teams to hear their points of view. As you can imagine, many of the same problems were highlighted by both groups, but they came at them from different angles, like a classic "he said, she said" scenario.

From my company's perspective, the project milestones were being hit and all of our commitments were on time, so there was complete bafflement on the part of our leaders as to why the client was unhappy. They kept trying to take some of the client leaders out for dinner or happy hours, but either they wouldn't go, or it wasn't helping the situation.

On the client side, there had been new leaders brought into key roles since the start of the program, and those leaders felt like my company was plowing ahead with delivery and not working with the new leaders. Worse, they felt like my company was blaming the new leaders every time something went wrong. They felt like they were being run over and dragged behind the program.

I had gotten agreement from the CFO to sit in a few meetings and observe to get a real feel for the team dynamics and interaction, without the "he said, she said" distortion.

I joined a meeting the CFO himself had set up to monitor the progress of the project. (The fact that the CFO had to set up the meeting was already an indication of a problem.) I was there as an observer and still wanted to crawl under the table because the meeting was so awkward. It was clear that both sides, including my company and the client teams, were trying to impress the CFO and neither side was working with the other below him. Status and details were raised in that meeting that had not been discussed with the other leaders previously, so both sides felt like they were getting ambushed.

After the meeting, I talked to the lead from my company and asked to see how governance was set up. It had been structured properly at the beginning of the program, with meetings at the junior levels before senior executive readouts, but as new leaders moved in, and after the CFO set up his own meeting, the governance cadence wasn't adjusted to match the new environment. And it was causing friction throughout the program.

I did the readout to the CFO and told him that we needed to adjust the governance, amongst other things. He nodded and later told my boss; governance was exactly the problem. It was right in front of them, but they were all too close to see it.

We changed the meeting cadences so that there was a meeting with the leaders below the CFO before his meeting, so that any issues could be raised and solved and status could be agreed upon before reading it out to the CFO. A leader from my company was assigned to each of the new leaders from the client company to work with them and bring them along on the project.

You may be rolling your eyes at how simple the fix was. Of course, there were a few additional changes needed beyond governance, and it wasn't a perfect program the next day. There was still a lot of work to be done to repair the damage that the friction had caused. Restructuring the meeting cadence was just the first step to ensure people stopped feeling ambushed. Then the team had to focus on the relationships and the collaboration, which was a longer-term process.

It was obvious to an outside observer what needed to be done. Super painfully obvious. But it's not always as obvious why the organization is unhealthy when you're in the middle of the fight. Especially if you're focused on addressing the symptoms of unhappiness and low morale, sometimes it's not so obvious that it's actually the bones that need shoring up.

Focusing on One Team, getting alignment on the WHAT, and restructuring the project to get the "bones" right, were all steps in the right direction. But there was still more to do in the endless uphill battle that was Project Ascend.

## LISTEN, LISTEN, LISTEN

I started Project Ascend the same way I started all of my recovery jobs, by spending the first week or two listening. I reached out to anyone on the team who I knew from previous work who might tell me the real deal. I met with some of the key leaders of the team, and I met with the key clients. I asked all of them very simple questions such as: What's working well with the program, and what's not working well? They were usually more than happy to tell me as much as I could stand about all of the problems that needed to be addressed.

I would also attend as many meetings as I could, including detailed lower-level status meetings as well as more senior executive reviews. In a meeting, you can see the interaction, feel the frustration, and understand the context without some of the blame or the "he said, she said" dynamic that you'll get when talking to clients or team members.

I had already spent a week listening and had started putting together my action plan when the CIO asked me to write up the list of all of the things wrong for him. I don't know how anyone could lead a team or do a recovery without taking the time to listen. Yet, it was immediately obvious that my predecessors hadn't listened to the SubCo team architects about what the software could do, versus a similar software that my company was more familiar with. My predecessors had assumed they knew and had made promises about what the software could do, and then they'd blamed the SubCo architects when the solution couldn't deliver what they'd promised.

I knew technologies enough to know that every software package was different, and I knew that I didn't know the software package that we were implementing. So, I asked the architects what it could do, what it couldn't do, and I made sure to double-check with them before I promised anything about its capabilities. Again, it seems so obvious, so simple . . . but it's a practice not always followed.

Here are a few other examples of how powerful a tool listening is for leaders, and how badly things can go when leaders don't listen to their teams.

## ask for options

One of the biggest mistakes a leader can make is telling the team what to do, or worse, telling the bosses or clients what will be done before finding out if it's feasible. So many leaders just assume the team will be able to make it happen.

I've watched leaders say to a boss or client that they'll give them the next version of a document by the next day without first asking the team how long the changes will take. Perhaps this seems insignificant, but it's an action that can quickly erode the trust of both the team, who will have to work through the night to get the document done, and the boss, if the material isn't to the level of quality desired because of lack of time to prepare.

I learned very early in my career, when I was the requirements lead for a system we were designing, to ask the team what was possible before making promises to others. My ideas on how to make the best system possible were only as good as the tech team lead (my peer) who would create my designs.

Whenever there was a need to do something that seemed nonstandard, I would discuss the need with the tech lead and ask her, "What are my options?" Once she understood the business need and what I was trying to do, she would offer a few things that could be done. I'd go with the one that seemed to best satisfy the business need and we'd continue forward.

As I continued in my career, I always asked the experts on my team what the technology could enable. I would ask the team for options and the solutions we were able to come up with as a result were much better. Even if you're the boss, you can't just order technology to do what you want. It just doesn't work that way. And though you might be able to order your team to do what you want, that will quickly break down trust and make it that much harder to achieve your overall goals.

## when we listened to the end users

Listening is especially important when designing a new system. And the group that most needs to be listened to are the people who will eventually use the system, who are called "end users" in the industry. Those are the accounting people who will use the accounting system, or the call center people who will have to answer the phones and use a system to create orders or resolve issues. If you don't understand the work those people are doing, and you aren't willing to listen, you shouldn't be designing a system for them. The same is true if you're designing a new process or giving the team a new direction, if you don't work with technology.

Early in my career, we were tasked with replacing an old system and building a new user interface. The old system was clunky and hard to use, and it required that users in call centers understand the ins and outs of both the system and the products that they were selling. The system couldn't stop people from making mistakes, so there were a lot of orders that failed, which cost time and money to re-enter correctly.

My company had been working with the clunky system for a while, and I was responsible for the design of the new system. I hadn't done anything like it, but I knew the system better than anyone else, having spent the previous year testing on it. I designed a prototype of the application the way I thought was the most logical based on my own understanding of the application.

When we had a prototype developed enough to tell the story of how the system would behave, we took it to the call center. We showed a group of call center representatives and supervisors how the system would be used and explained the processes they would have to follow.

Then we listened to their feedback.

They told us what they liked about it and what we had gotten wrong. Because the system was just a mock-up at that point, we could change things around quickly. There were some more challenging requests they gave us, which we brainstormed overnight. The next day we showed them the revisions to make sure the solution we'd come up with addressed the issues they'd raised.

One of the most interesting things about that project is that the morale level in the call center increased simply because we had visited, and because we had listened to their feedback, even before the new system was rolled out.

And after the system was released, it was one of the most successful projects ever at that client. It met the original business case (which was purely because it reduced the number of servers), but it exceeded expectations on so many other levels. It reduced training time from *weeks* to *hours*, reduced errors and order failures, and increased representative engagement. The fact that we had listened and adapted our design to the day-to-day work of the representatives made all the difference.

## when we didn't listen to the end users

After our success on the call center project, we always tried to meet with the end users. But I've participated on numerous jobs in which we were not allowed to talk to end users. We've offered, asked, begged, and have often been told no. The reasons have been varied, but the result has never been positive, certainly not as positive as the project where we spent time and really understood the day-to-day lives of the users.

On Project Ascend, the business clients wouldn't let us talk to the end users. We asked, we begged, and they said, "There is no need." They said that they (the business stakeholders) came from the field and "understood the day-to-day jobs of the field workers," so they were able to give us all of the requirements and there was no need to get the field workers' input.

Even if the business clients were 100 percent right about the requirements, because of how well they understood the field worker's lives (which was utterly not true), they missed a chance to listen to the field workers, to show them that their opinions mattered, and to demonstrate that the system was being designed *for them.*

They didn't listen to the field workers, and when the design that they'd come up with actually made the field worker's lives harder there was a mass protest, and no one would use the system. There were attempts to adjust the system, but ultimately the field workers rejected it, and it was scrapped. That scenario is obviously an extreme example, but it's not unheard of, and it's definitely not the result the clients were looking for in a system.

Project Ascend's requirements were driven by the different stakeholder organizations, each of whom had an entirely different objective, from replicating their current legacy system to replacing their mainframes to gathering more data. It was a clear case of no one listening to anyone else. Everyone had different goals, and no one cared to listen to anyone else's goals.

And most importantly, none of them cared to listen to the people who would ultimately be using the system. None of them asked what the end users needed or what they wanted the system to do.

## the value of listening

When I was first brought in on Project Triad, I did the same thing I always did. I spent time with various team members to understand what was working and what wasn't. I had worked with a few people on the team before, so I made a point to set up time to meet with them and understand from their perspective what was going wrong in the hopes they would tell me the unvarnished truth.

The people I talked to told me that the previous three or four leaders had just jumped in and started telling the team what to do. One of the consistent themes I heard from the team was that the previous leaders had "dictated" to them, telling them to do things, even if there were better, more efficient, or more effective ways of proceeding.

The team was working nights, weekends, and eighteen-hour days, and they were definitely not as productive as they could have been. They were burned out, run down, run over, and they weren't doing things the way they would normally have done.

Honestly, just doing the absolute bare minimum of hearing their concerns made a noticeable improvement, even before I had time to implement any changes. Simply feeling listened to made a huge difference in their morale.

Though I didn't begin the Project Ascend case study with this section on "Listening," it was definitely my first focus, and it formed the basis for all of the changes I needed to make on Project Ascend, including reforming our team into One Team, reassessing governance, and resetting our team's objectives.

Once I got through that first set of changes I started to see there was another major issue, an elephant in the room, that was a separate source of our problems.

## BULLY CULTURE AND OTHER CHALLENGING CULTURES

On Project Ascend, after I'd made the first round of improvements, like fixing the governance, and once I had gotten the team to start working as a single team, I thought there would be no more yelling. I thought the clients had only been yelling because things were so badly screwed up.

While there had been a reduction in the yelling, it definitely hadn't stopped. They would still yell at us whenever they wanted us to do something, especially when we tried to push back. They were bullying the team to get what they wanted, even if that wasn't the right answer.

I couldn't understand why they would still bully our team when we'd made so many changes.

Then I realized it wasn't just our team.

The company employees would bully each other as well. If one of the junior clients said something couldn't be done in the desired timeframe, the senior clients would just yell and threaten and yell more until they agreed to the more aggressive timeline, which would not be met because it was unrealistic. And then, when the timeline wasn't met, the senior clients would yell more. It was eye-opening, really, and I couldn't understand why anyone worked at that company. Who would want to live in an environment like that?

I could fix the dynamics between our team and the client team, but fix the entire corporate culture? That wasn't something I was going to change, so I had to figure out how to manage the project within it.

The Project Ascend client also did what I called "theater." I'd never seen anything quite like it in all of the companies I'd worked at. I'd go to my stakeholder and discuss an issue and how to resolve it. We'd come to a good agreement about how to proceed, and it would be a nice, amiable, solution-oriented meeting. And then I'd go into a meeting an hour later, where there were ten people, and the same individual I'd just had a nice discussion with would be yelling and screaming at me. To my face, they might've said, "Absolutely, I understand that the requirements you're being given don't make sense. We need to get the business group in line." Then less than an hour later, in a staff meeting with the business representatives, the very same person would say, "You need to give the business what they need! Anything else is unacceptable." It was enough to give me whiplash.

The first time it happened to me, it was like I'd stepped into the twilight zone. Did the person forget? No, it was all an act. They couldn't be seen to be nice or they'd lose all credibility with their peers in the bullying-yelling-escalating culture.

My pragmatic, straightforward, transparent nature had a hard time with that one. Maybe I should have had some sort of "the consultant fights back" face on, or a script prepared . . . but that just wasn't me.

They had proven that they would escalate, escalate, and escalate again until they got what they wanted, regardless of the truth. If you find yourself in this situation, here are a few suggestions.

There may be someone in the organization who is reasonable and senior enough to address the situation; if so, build a relationship with them, and work with them to solve the challenges. In this case, my boss had a very good relationship with the CFO, and they could work though things rationally behind the scenes and sometimes resolve the situation.

You should also try to avoid being in situations where there will be an opportunity for others to gang up on you. Avoid large meetings and try to get things resolved one-on-one. Make sure to get signatures there, so the agreed plans stick. (I'll talk more about this in the "No Blame; Just Solutions" section, next.)

Pre-escalate. Sometimes, the only way to manage a bully is to out-bully them. Pre-escalate and get your message out to the leadership before they have a chance to get theirs published.

If the bully culture is too crazy for you, get someone in who can out-crazy them. I'll also cover "out-crazying" in more detail later in the "No Blame; Just Solutions" section.

## faux nice

One other company culture I encountered and had a hard time navigating was "faux nice," what they themselves actually called "company nice" aka passive aggressive. For example, in meetings or one-on-one discussions, someone is totally nice and calm with you and tells you things are going well, while on the backend they're working internally to figure out how to cancel your project, or they're escalating to the CIO or CTO that they're not happy with the program or with your performance. Again, it wasn't just the consultant team that had to deal with this. The client's own culture was that way, so even the company employees within their own teams had to be on guard against being smiled at and backstabbed.

You'd think a culture that is nice would be easier than a bully culture. At least they're nice to you and not screaming at you. But, similar to how the overt discrimination I'd faced in the military had been easier to deal with than the subtle unconscious biases I faced in the corporate world, at least you know what you're up against in a bully culture. At least you know their position when they're screaming and blaming you for everything (unless the screaming is "theatre," like I mentioned earlier).

Faux nice is hard to protect against, if you don't even know there is a back channel against you. I have encountered those clients a few times and the best you can do is make the strongest relationships possible with as many people as possible at the most senior levels possible. You do so, hoping that one of them will be a coach and tell you what is really happening so that you can figure out what to do. Or you build relationships in the hope that someone senior enough will protect you from the blow if it comes.

I debated including the bully culture in with the discussion on "No Blame; Just Solutions" because there is usually an element of blame in anyone who is a bully. Bullies redirect the blame away from themselves, even if, or especially if, they are 100 percent at fault.

But ultimately, I decided to keep the topics of bullying and blaming separate because while they are related, there is essentially a Venn diagram with some parts between bullying and blaming overlapping and some parts being unique.

Bullies push to get what they want, which really has nothing to do with blame until things go wrong, and then they blame you, even when you told them that what they're asking for is not the best solution.

Blame can also happen without bullying, where people can simply redirect the blame, in a duck-and-cover move, without the aggressive intimidation of a bully.

In Project Ascend, because it was both a bullying culture and a blame culture, the bully circle and the blame circle of the Venn diagram were almost completely overlapped, and it made for an especially challenging environment.

## NO BLAME; JUST SOLUTIONS

On Project Ascend, almost immediately upon my arrival I had pulled out my Guiding Principles, especially focusing on One Team and No Blame; Just Solutions.

"No Blame" can seem almost counterintuitive. It would've been so easy, so natural, to point at the other team, or the other guy, and say it's their fault. Not ours, not mine. But it never works that way. Especially in a complex environment, like Project Ascend, there is very rarely only a single issue, and there is often a matter of interpretation in terms of what happened and what should have been done. And once blame starts, that blame-casting and finger-pointing can whip around an organization, breaking down teamwork, and limiting an organization's ability to get things done when everyone is afraid of catching blame. I have never seen a culture of "blame" be a healthy one.

Once I rolled out the No Blame; Just Solutions guiding principle, I had to live up to it and support it, both within my team, including my company and the SubCo, as well as across the client company. It wasn't until later that I realized what a bully and blame culture I was walking into, which was the corporate culture. It was not just a problem with the team or the project.

## blame breaks trust; trust breaks apart blame

It didn't take long for the "No Blame; Just Solutions" principle to be tested by my team, both from my company and SubCo. While the teamwork between our companies was getting better, the relationship with the client was still rocky. We had to negotiate a new contract to cover the additional time the work would take to be done and the client was trying to rake us over the coals and add penalties on every line of the contract. Of course, they believed that we were at fault (at least they aggressively acted as if we were) for the work having taken so long, so they felt the penalties were justified. It was a brutal negotiation.

After literally months of negotiations, we were down to the final clauses and hoped to get the contract signed within the week. And that was right when my team brought to my attention a security vulnerability in the system we'd been developing. Alarms were going off in my head. They would blame us for security issues. This would stop the contract. We were going to be kicked out.

I wanted to know how it had happened, how we could have been so careless. I couldn't blame my team though, or I would immediately erode any trust I'd started to build with them. And blame wouldn't help anyway. We just had to solve it.

I took a deep breath, and said, "Show me." My team walked me through what the vulnerability was, and thankfully it was not as bad as it could have been. It would take an experienced and dedicated hacker to know what to do, and then the data they would uncover was only business addresses, not sensitive personal data. It was still a security vulnerability. It still had to be resolved quickly, but it could have been worse.

I asked, "What are our options for solving it?" The architect and the developer who found it, to their credit, had already been thinking through options. The options were essentially to do an overnight patch, or to wait a week and solve it in a more architecturally solid way, or both. If we did the patch, we would have to advise our client. If we did the better solution in a week we might be able to slip it into an already-planned release and they wouldn't be any the wiser. But that wasn't the right thing to do. And if they ever found out we'd had a security vulnerability and didn't tell them, they'd never trust us again.

The thought of telling the client was like having to get open-heart surgery with no anesthesia, but not telling them wasn't an option. I had to tell them.

I texted my client that I needed to talk to him and walked up the stairs to his office. I told him, providing as much detail as I could regarding the problem and our recommendation to fix it.

Instead of the blame I expected, he was very calm and said, "This is what we expect out of the partnership. We want you to tell us what we need to know, even if it's difficult. You're the experts, not us, so you need to tell us."

Resetting the standards for trust and blame had empowered my team to tell me a hard truth. And I had to respond calmly and not blame them or it would've been the last time they brought me anything. I then had to swallow all of the alarm bells going off in my head to tell my client. And, because he knew how hard it was for me to bring it to him in the middle of our negotiations, he saw it as a sign of trust and didn't hold it against us. It actually improved the relationship and built trust.

We jointly agreed on a plan to remediate the problem, and we moved forward.

## just solutions

On Project Ascend, when we finally got the contract signed, we had a ton of documents to produce for every stage in the delivery lifecycle. Way more than most projects. We had whittled the list of documents down during the contract negotiations, but it still ended up being a lot.

The problem was not so much producing the documents; I had a whole team that would do a lot of these documents as part of their normal delivery process. The bigger challenge was getting someone from the client team to read and approve them. And we also weren't doing a great job tracking and logging those approvals.

I had put someone on my team in charge of the document approval process, and we had come up with the basics of how approvals would be tracked. But there was a lot going on, and my team wasn't keeping up with it. I, as the leader, should have been paying more attention to how it was going, but I wasn't focused on it either.

It got escalated to my boss that we were far behind on our deliverables. The way the client worded the escalation, they made it appear as if we hadn't done our deliverables (which put the blame on us), when the problem was really a combination of issues. We were probably behind on some documents; they hadn't signed off on some, and we weren't tracking and managing the process as well as we should have. It made the problem look worse than it was. The clients at Project Ascend were masters at escalations, master bullies, and they generally weren't concerned about the truth.

When my boss called me and told me about the escalation, I was working from home because I felt horrible. I was sitting on the couch, in a sleeping bag, shivering and feverish. We were already in an escalation firestorm and the client was adding fuel to the fire, trying to make us look as bad as possible, because that's what they did.

After I hung up with my boss, I texted Brian, who was the lead responsible for the document process. I asked him to get the other members of the document team and call me. A few minutes later Brian had gathered everyone into a conference room and called. I was upset. I looked stupid in front of my boss. I was sick, and I was angry. And this job was so miserable because the clients were just awful to us. I wanted to yell.

But I knew that wouldn't help. And I knew that it was as much my fault for not paying attention to the documents as it was anyone else's. I took a deep breath, and said calmly: "What percentage of documents are currently complete and approved?"

There was complete silence, and then Brian said, "We'll need to calculate that and get back to you."

"Do we have a dashboard or document showing what has been delivered, what is pending approval, or what is approved?"

"We haven't been tracking it at that level of detail."

"The clients are escalating that we are behind on our documents. My guess is that we have done a lot of them, but we aren't focused on getting reviews and approvals. Because of that it looks like we're far behind. We need to be able to show them our status in detail, and we need to focus on getting anything outstanding done, plus get approvals on what we've finished."

Brian said, "We'll start working on pulling it together."

"Let me know what I can do to help. I'm happy to review the draft dashboard or tracker to make sure it has all of the information we need. Let's check in tomorrow and see how far it is."

We hung up, and I curled down into the sleeping bag. I was not feeling well, and this did not help at all.

Months later, after we'd gotten our documents done and as the project was ending, Brian told me, "I knew how upset you were. We had dropped the ball! But it meant so much that instead of getting angry and yelling at us, as you had every right to do, you worked on it with us."

I had forgotten that specific incident until he brought it back up, and I appreciated that feedback because there had been times I'd questioned myself. *Would the team be more effective if I would just get mad and yell sometimes?* Certainly, a lot of my colleagues would just demand results and get angry. I have wondered if my way of working through things together is always the right way, or whether there are times that some anger is needed.

Maybe. But that's not who I am and that's not how I chose to lead. If the objective of a leader is to build a team to get a job done, then anger wouldn't help. I believe anger breaks down a team, and anger doesn't help to solve problems. Stay calm, don't blame, and focus on the solution to get the job done.

## fix the process, not the person

If your first question when your team brings a problem to you is, "Who did it?" it may be the last time your team brings you a problem. And yet, I hear that question "Who?" so many times from my bosses and clients.

We had an incident when we were managing systems for a client on a later project. The systems were extremely outdated and fragile, and while we had been slowly working to improve the processes and reduce the amount of errors, there was only so much we could do with these house-of-cards systems. One evening when a file failed to run, our team member followed the processes to get the file to run again, but he made a mistake and used an old file. The real-life consequences of that were to have hundreds of customers get double-billed by the company. It took the customer reps all of the next day to back out those charges for the customers. It was a serious issue.

Our client was rightly upset and we were in his office first thing in the morning. "Who did it?" he asked. "I want them gone!" he said. He could be a bully, and the team was afraid of him. Especially when he was angry.

We had done our homework before we stepped into the office, so we understood the situation and what had happened. "Who?" was not the right question to ask.

The problem is that anyone can make a mistake. And if everyone is so afraid to make a mistake, no one is going to want to do the work. Or, they are going to be so afraid to be found out that they'll blame others, hide what happened, and not be open about the possible fixes.

We explained what had happened. The person followed the process but had used an old file. The person was a good worker who had done this job many, many times and had executed it flawlessly, they just made a mistake. What we needed to do was change the process to limit the chance of there being any future errors. We added a step in the process that anytime the failure happened, the person had to call in a supervisor to double check the steps and the file before executing, so that there would be a second set of eyes on the process.

We documented the new process, made sure all of the supervisors and team knew it, and we never had a repeat of that problem.

If we had simply focused on the "who," we would have lost a good team member, and it would have put the rest of the team on edge that they could be next if they made an error. It also wouldn't have fixed the underlying process which would leave an opening for another error. It also would have shown the team that we, as their leaders, would not back them up if they did anything wrong, and it might even make them think about quitting. It was a stressful environment already, so if they thought they could be rolled off for making one mistake while working on these house-of-cards systems, why would they stay?

## compliment-cast

One of the best, and somewhat counterintuitive, ways of stopping blame-casting is to compliment other parties or organizations when they do something well.

Again, if the whole reason for blame-casting is to duck blame and cast it on someone else, then compliment-casting seems counterintuitive. If you're being blamed *and* you're complimenting who is blaming you, then they could look doubly better than you.

But the same way blame will zip around an organization, the principle of reciprocity says that if you compliment someone for a job well done, they'll do the same when they see you doing something well.

## be fact-based and neutral

If you are in a situation with multiple parties and where blame is in the air, one of the best defenses is to be fact-based and neutral-toned. This is harder than it sounds, as the other parties in the discussion may be lobbing accusations that are either untrue or based on single anecdotes that paint the picture they want it to show.

To be prepared for those discussions, do your research and make sure you understand the real facts of the case. Push your team to get to the root cause and the details. Ask them what the opposition would say, so that you're as prepared as possible. Don't forget that the team may not want to look bad in front of you, and they may not be as open as you want them to be. Don't just ask them for the story because you may only get their version of events without all of the layers. Probe for the details until you have a good understanding of what really happened.

After we'd experienced a major issue with our code deployments on Project Ascend, which had kept us from being able to deliver code to production for about two months (It was a big deal!), the client asked for a root cause analysis (RCA). They wanted an understanding of what had gone wrong, why, and it needed to be detailed. RCAs are typically super detailed, with timelines and seven levels of "why".

For example: Why did the accident happen? Because the blue car swerved into the red car's lane. Why? Because the blue car swerved to avoid a raccoon. Why? Because the raccoon ran across the road. Why? Because there is no wildlife crossing. Why? You get the point.

I asked my tech lead to work with the team on it. He said, "Will do!" And I could immediately see there was no way it was going to get done, not to the level I needed, and not to the point that I would understand it all.

Why did I think that? I'd already been asking for a write-up of what had happened and so far hadn't gotten anything. And this needed to be detailed, not a high-level write-up. In my experience, super technical people either don't write well (they are wired for numbers, calculations, and equations, and writing narratives can be challenging), or they write in such super technical language that I'd have to parse out each sentence and try to make sense of it in order to communicate to my clients. Since I was the one that was going to have to face the firing squad, I needed to understand it.

I asked my tech lead to pull together a meeting with four or five of our key technical architects, and I pulled in one of our entry-level analysts to help me document. Then I started interviewing the team, starting with what happened, and then asking When, What, How, Why, Why, Why, Why questions until we got down to what we believed really happened. I was like a crime scene detective digging in.

From my point of view there were multiple factors involved. First, the fast-paced development environment meant the client demanded a lot of changes and they were not open to waiting for a change to go in, even if there was an issue happening. The client's bully culture meant they would yell and escalate and escalate again until the team did what they wanted, even if the correct course of action would have been to wait the time needed to resolve an issue.

The bully culture made my team less likely to raise their hands and tell the client that there was an issue that would delay a deployment to the test environment. Some of this happened before I arrived, but some of it continued once I was there, because the team had been conditioned that way and I didn't realize what was happening or that it could cause problems.

Secondly, the software we were using was less robust (at that time) in its code deployment mechanisms, and there were some product software bugs that made deployments challenging.

And lastly, my team manipulated the system to get the code to deploy when they hit the product bugs, and that led to some scrambled, broken pieces in the system which got worse and worse until the code wouldn't deploy.

When we finished writing up the RCA, I had gone through it in detail with both the software vendor representative, Shawn, and the lead IT client, Linda, to make sure that all three of us agreed with what was being presented. All three companies, including mine, the software vendor, and the client would be represented in the read-out of the RCA. We needed to be aligned and have the same story. All three entities had contributed to the challenges and the result: the client with the bully culture, the vendor with the product bugs, and my team, by pushing the code instead of calling a halt.

What should have happened is the details of the RCA would have been covered in a fact-based neutral manner, at a meeting with relevant leadership, as requested. There would have been questions to answer, of course, but since the software vendor representative, the client IT lead, and I had all aligned on the message, we would have had the same story to tell and would have been able to address all of our leaders' questions.

However, that's not what happened, which brings me to the last point in this "No Blame; Just Solutions" section.

## don't assume the other guys will always play nice

Linda, the client IT lead, had set up the meeting for a Monday morning, and I had initially been told that it would be later in the week. "Don't worry," she said, "this is just a casual, preliminary read-out. It's just a conversation."

But I knew it wasn't, not when I saw that the CIO, CFO, all of the IT leadership, and all of my leadership had been invited.

I should have known I was in for an ambush. I also should have known that despite how much time we had all spent jointly preparing the story, and jointly agreeing, that in front of their bosses Monday morning the others' story would change.

We were no longer in reality; we were now in a "theater," and they were reading from the *Blame Tauni's Team* script, and I still had the script of *These Are the Facts and We All Played a Part in the Challenges*.

Shawn, the software vendor, brought up points (allegations?) in the meeting that he had never raised to me before. And this was after he had told me to my face that the real root of the problem was the software. He had told me numerous times it was a product problem and we should not be held liable. More theater!

Linda said it was all our fault in so many different ways. And these people, with whom I had directly spoken about these challenges and the facts around them, were now looking at me, lying to my face, and putting on the biggest show of their lives.

I was not prepared for that. I was prepared to be on trial with facts. I wasn't prepared for abject lies. I maintained my calm and continued to provide the facts of the case, but this discussion was not about facts. Whoever was at fault was going to have to pay for the delays, so everyone was trying to blame us and avoid paying.

What I should have done is call my bosses the night before the meeting. We should have arranged to skip the meeting and pushed to reschedule it with a smaller audience, or I should have let one of my bosses negotiate. There was no way that meeting was ever going to be fair.

But I never would have predicted that the meeting would be that bad. We had all aligned on the message! We had agreed! I just couldn't imagine that the clients and the vendor would be so awful as to prepare the message with me and then just lie.

If fair and honest is a 0 on the crazy scale, I could maybe imagine a level 5 of crazy and I could be prepared to defend against it. I could maybe even imagine a level 10 crazy scenario, but I'd consider it just as remote as preparing for an invasion from Mars. However, at this meeting the clients came in with a 15 or a 25 on the crazy scale, well beyond my scale of imagination and comprehension.

On one of my earlier projects, the client had been similarly crazy with the truth. We kept preparing for level 10 insanity and the client would bring level 25. My first boss was a lot like me and kept expecting the client to be fair-ish. He kept getting blindsided and the client would get the upper hand and the project would suffer.

After he retired, the second boss was much better at bringing the crazy. He would assume that the client would be level 25 crazy, so we would prepare a level 35 crazy response. He was amazing at out-crazying the client. It was something I could never, ever do.

As a quick example, if an issue had occurred like the one on Project Ascend, a reasonable person might expect that each involved organization had a hand in the issue, so the cost of the repair might be split between them. That is what I had been assuming on this RCA. All three of us had a hand in it, so all three of us were partially liable. There might be some negotiation on the percentage of liability, but not on our mutual fault.

When similar issues happened where both parties were involved at my old project, my old boss would assume they would be fair and be prepared to negotiate each party's level of responsibility. Was it 50/50? Or 60/40? The craziest scenario he could imagine is that they would push for a 70/30 split.

But that client would say it was 100 percent our fault, and we needed to fix it all for free, plus throw in some additional work for free, plus bake them an apple pie (ok, not the pie).

My new boss, he would go in assuming that the client would ask for 100 percent from us, but he would have a counteroffer that was even crazier. He would be ready to say they were 100 percent at fault, so they should pay us for all of the work we'd have to do to fix it. *Plus* they should pay for the twenty extra people we'd have to bring on, *plus* they'd have to give us new work, *plus* they'd have to give us a chocolate fountain while we work. Because he was prepared for the 100 percent-plus-the-chocolate-fountain conversation, he was better positioned to negotiate that client into more of a 50/50 position.

So, if you are assuming your client or boss will be fair, and they won't be, be prepared for the craziest possible response and be ready to out-crazy, or at least equally-crazy, them.

Or, if you're like me, and you just don't think that way, get help from someone who can play the game and can one-up the crazy. Don't be afraid to bring on someone who, either by experience or disposition, can get to level 35 crazy.

While I still believe fact-based and neutral is the right way to handle things 98 percent of the time, I still anticipate that people will be crazy 2 percent of the time. Be careful, or you'll be blindsided.

The corporate culture where we did Project Ascend made the project uniquely challenging. The technology we were working on was also a challenge and contributed to our problems (Regardless of what Shawn said in the RCA!).

I had to not only focus on building up the team, but I had to manage the client and get a deep understanding of the technology.

It took a while, but things finally started to turn around and I could feel the team starting to gel. The project was finally starting to get where I wanted.

## WHAT IS A STRONG TEAM?

On Project Ascend, after what felt like a monumental amount of work, and finding and fixing all of the puzzle pieces to build a team, we got to a point that started to feel relatively good to me. But I wanted to make sure that the team also felt the change.

I approached a few people on the team who I knew would be the toughest critics and asked, "On a scale of 0 to 100, how does the team feel?" The people I asked had been on my previous projects or were the people I had built some trust with. I expected complete honesty from them. I also picked people of differing levels and roles so that the answers would be as representative of the whole team as possible.

But they needed some definition in the scale, like what 0 looks like, what 100 should look like.

I know a good team when I see one, but everyone's understanding of "good" may be different. They may measure it based on one of the better teams they'd been part of, which may not be the same as what I was trying to achieve in the team.

So, I came up with these three criteria for what "good" looks like in a team. A good team should:

**Meet the milestones/commitments on time/on budget.** Meeting the team's outcomes, the WHAT, is still a mandatory minimum, otherwise there is still brokenness in the team or in the environment, even if the team is happy.

**Fire on all cylinders.** This may be harder to define, but it can be gauged in a few ways. First, the team is able to operate without friction. The team is able to churn out work, with everyone knowing who does what and how to accomplish tasks. Everyone understands their role and how they fit into the overall working of the team. There are no silos that make communication hard. People's roles don't overlap and cause unnecessary competition. There are no major gaps in the team that people have to compensate for, and no bottlenecks where everything has to route through a single person. Finally, there aren't so many meetings or administrative hurdles that it feels like nothing can get done.

**It feels like a family.**[1] The most subjective "criteria" of all. What does "feels like a family" mean to me? Being a family is having a strong sense of camaraderie. Is everyone willing to help each other? Do people joke together and do people eat together at lunch or go out for dinner or drinks after work (the latter is especially true when people are traveling for work). Are there cliques in the team, where some are "in" and others are excluded, or does everyone have a sense of belonging? Do people count on each other, not blame each other, and not talk about people behind their backs, or is there an undercurrent of dislike and distrust running through the team?

Understanding that these criteria were still very subjective, the people I asked had enough sense of what I was looking for to give me a number. The first time I asked, I got numbers in the 40s. It was like a punch in the gut. A few of the overly optimistic people (or those who wanted to be nice) gave the team 60s. I discarded the 60s and knew that 40 was probably the real experience of the team. I had been hoping for scoring in the 70s. I realized I still had a long way to go. I may have cleaned up the big roadblocks, but we still had a very rocky road ahead of us.

Of course it wasn't about the number. The number itself was meaningless and purely subjective. When they told me their number, then I could ask why. What are the gaps and issues they're still seeing? There were many reasons why we weren't at 100 yet. I took notes on all of their reasons and then worked over the next weeks and months to see where we could make further improvements.

When I felt like we'd made progress again, whether it was in a week or a quarter, I'd randomly ask a few people on the team what our number was. I noticed there was a gradual rise from scores in the 40s to the 60s to the 70s. We weren't where I wanted to be yet, and there were still things that we needed to work on, but there was a definite improvement.

Several months later, we had a team party celebrating the completion of one of the major releases. A few people on the team volunteered to set it up. They said they wanted a karaoke machine, and I thought, *Who in the world is going to sing?* They also wanted a photo booth. The cost wasn't that bad, so I agreed to it, but I imagined that we'd mostly just have dinner and those wouldn't get much use.

I was very wrong.

The photo booth was in constant use, with three, four, or five people cramming in at a time, with silly hats and glasses as props adding to the fun. Each photo showed a cross-section of the team, across teams, across companies (my company and SubCo), across genders, and across levels. There was an endless array of photos taken in the booth.

When karaoke was announced after dinner, I held my breath to see what would happen. One of the junior members of the team took the stage and knocked us all over with his rendition of Celine Dion's "My Heart Will Go On," which was amazing. I thought, *No way is anyone going to want to follow that act,* but one of the women started grabbing the other women across levels and companies and got us to sing, "We

Are Family." And the songs never stopped, usually group singing, usually a combination of people that crossed the org chart, including my boss, who had come for the event.

I make it a policy to never to do an afterparty, because it usually goes too late, there is often too much alcohol involved, and I am a morning person, so I like to be at the office by 7:00 a.m. at the latest, while at that project it was usually closer to 6:30 a.m. But no one wanted this party to stop. We found a bar nearby where there was dancing involved (Thankfully there are no pictures of that!), and then a gaggle of us wandered over to the hotel where one of the team members had gotten a suite that week because of his hotel status.

At around 2:00 a.m., about fifteen of us were crowded around a dining room table in the hotel suite. We were all just hanging out and talking. The moment was memorialized and the photos were passed around the next day. A SubCo team member had taken the pictures and sent them out with "Family," as the subject line. There were people of every level, gender, age, and technology background, from both my company and the SubCo.

That moment in the hotel suite was the real answer to my question. We had finally achieved the team I wanted.

Once the team is strong, if each of the criteria are met, the team should essentially be able to run itself. If the leader has to have a hand in everything to make it run, that's not a strong team. With a strong team, the leader should be able to focus on the more strategic things coming their way, like bringing new products to the team or selling new projects. Or the leader should potentially be able take on additional teams. Until the team is strong, their entire focus should be getting the team to gel and deliver.

Once the teams I worked with were "fixed" and the teams were strong, it was usually time for me to take on the next team and let a junior leader step up and take over the previous team. In the case of Project Ascend, we were able to complete the project and we all left together.

On Project Ascend, there were so many puzzle pieces I had to put together to get the team strong. I had to get the team working as One Team and remove the silos and the blame. I had to work with the client to get the WHAT clarified so that the team wasn't working on competing objectives. And I had to build in the basic discipline and governance so that we weren't constantly reinventing status and making decisions without all of the key players in the room.

It was the hardest project I'd ever fixed, in the most challenging environment. The people from that team are still some of my best friends and most trusted colleagues. We went through fire together there, and I would entrust my life to them.

3.

# FAST BUT NOT FURIOUS: PROJECT BLAST CASE STUDY

Project Blast was an entirely different kind of project from everything I'd done in the past. The best part was that it wasn't a recovery. However, I was brought in because it was going to be extremely challenging, and it would quickly turn into a recovery if it wasn't done right. We were supposed to have a six-month timeline to complete the project, which would have been extremely tight, but the contract was signed late, so we were down to only *five* months.

In those five months, we had to launch a brand-new website with strong cyber security, provide training documents, and be ready to support the site on an ongoing basis from the day it launched. When I say, "brand-new," I'm not kidding. We literally had to create this website out of thin air. Usually for projects, we would leverage a client's existing IT environment and build into it or connect to it, but in this case our "client" was a consortium of different companies, and we were building the website on the cloud to serve all of their companies. This was literally from scratch.

There were also a lot of crazy constraints in the contract that would make this project not just a sprint, but a sprint over an obstacle course laden with mines. Not only did we have to complete the project on time, or face penalties, and not only did we have to get the security right or face massive fines for security issues, but we had crazy milestones we had to hit in the middle of the timeline. We had to do a user acceptance test at three and a half months, and we had to do a beta test at four and a half months. This beta test, which wasn't clearly defined, would require our website to be used by industry insiders. All of this meant that we had to have the software ready and running well by the three-and-a-half-month point, and basically ready to launch by four and a half months.

And, the last straw that made this project just feel like it was going to go off the rails before we even started, was that leadership from my company had gotten onstage alongside consortium leaders at an industry event and announced to the world that we were launching this website and when it would launch.

There was no chance of slipping the date. It would hurt both our reputation, because we'd announced it publicly, and our pockets, because we would be fined in the contract for every day we slipped. The consortium's reputation was on the line as well, which is why they'd put those fines into the contract.

This is what I walked into when I was asked to lead Project Blast. Fortunately, there were a handful of people already staffed, including the Product Owner who would essentially become my right-hand man.

However, I knew that with only five months, I needed to have all of the right people, and only the right people.

## THE RIGHT PEOPLE

One of the primary principles author Jim Collins shares in his leadership book, *Good to Great*, is: "Get the right people on the bus." The basic assumption is that being with the right team of "A" players will enable you to accomplish anything. I think the principle can be true in certain circumstances, and I've seen some amazing executives move around to different roles in companies and be successful in all of them because of it.

However, in my experience, there are times when you absolutely need to have the right skills. No amount of "greatness" will make up for lack of skills. If your bus full of football players is driving to a basketball game, you're destined to lose the game. I don't care if they're all-star football players. They'd lose against real basketball players.

## specific skills are needed

On Project Blast, the first thing I did was meet with anyone who had already been brought on board, focusing on those who would play lead roles.

I met with one guy who droned on for thirty minutes about his amazing career working on old-style technology, but he had never worked on the cloud. He said he could learn quickly but I wasn't sure how he could learn if he never listened. I needed collaboration. I needed skills. I didn't need his attitude.

After I'd met with everyone, I ended up rolling five people off. That may not sound like a lot, but it was five out of about twenty, so I had to staff-up the remaining roles quickly so we could start strong.

Because I was a fixer and I worked on different technologies, I couldn't just bring a set of strong people with me wherever I went. Most of the folks I'd worked with in past projects worked on specific software packages and their skills didn't apply to Project Blast, which was cloud native.

The other factor was that my company hadn't done that many cloud native website builds at the time. It was a newer technology, and we didn't have that many people in the company who'd built websites like that.

I spent the first week searching for people with the right skills and bringing them on. I found a layer of experienced leaders who were experts in their areas, including security architecture, cloud native architecture, and user interface design and build. Then there was a vast gap where I couldn't find any mid-level people with the specific skills needed.

I finally brought on five or six entry-level employees, analysts who had no particular skills except for a huge willingness to jump in and learn, and I paired them up with the experienced leaders.

I paired one analyst who had a more technical college degree with the cloud native architect who essentially apprenticed him for the project. I aligned the product owner with several analysts who were responsible for defining the user stories, and one of them became the scrum master, organizing and managing our agile work.

Each of these analysts contributed to the program in an outsized way, which might lead some to say we had the right people on the bus; to claim they were A+ players regardless of the game.

It's true that we had A+ players, but without skilled players (our experienced leaders) to guide those players it would have been a disaster.

For example, consider Melissa. She was part of the functional team and had been writing user stories under the guidance of our experienced product owner. When I asked if she could start preparing for user acceptance testing (UAT), she said, "Absolutely! What is UAT?" (User Acceptance Testing, or UAT, is testing completed by end users on a system prior to it being put into production.)

In this particular contract we had to pass UAT with a 100 percent pass rate. It's not something that is usually done, as there are always errors and nothing is ever 100 percent. But those who had signed this contract had decided that 100 percent was okay by us, and so I had to figure out how to get us through it.

Melissa was eager and smart as a whip, but she didn't even know what UAT was much less how to prepare for it. And she certainly didn't know how to protect us against penalties if we didn't hit the 100 percent requirement.

I walked her through what I wanted and explained how I wanted to run UAT. With the product owner's support, she got the testing scenarios documented. We controlled UAT with an iron fist and managed to get the 100 percent pass rate, which was a minor miracle. She and the other analysts that were working with her did a great job, but without my coaching and the product owner's guidance, she wouldn't have even known how to get started.

In another instance, after I had gotten agreement from a training expert to join the project, Melissa strode over to my desk and said, "Can I help with training?" I let her help, and she essentially apprenticed to the training expert once he joined. She did an amazing job on that as well.

No doubt Melissa was a great resource for the team, and there were multiple other entry-level analysts who were just as amazing and without whom we wouldn't have been able to do the project. However, if I'd only had entry-level resources, we would have been sunk.

You can't put a person like Melissa into the role of a security architect, no matter how great and eager they are. She wouldn't have been able to do UAT or training or user stories without someone experienced to coach and guide her.

You can have them work under the direction of an experienced person, and that will both give the experienced person leverage and allow the junior person to soak up knowledge. Just having great people isn't enough—you need skilled people, and you need the right people in those skilled roles.

Once we had the right team, we had to get the design of the system figured out quickly so that we could get it built.

We couldn't lose a single moment of the project on something like misaligned objectives, as we'd experienced on Project Ascend, or on ill-defined requirements. We needed to figure out the design and get to coding.

## CRITICAL THINKING: REVERSE *JEOPARDY*

On Project Ascend, one of our biggest problems was that the client didn't know what they wanted. The IT leadership wanted an MVP, minimal viable product, but they couldn't define what that meant. They had no clear understanding of what the MVP needed to do. They would make hopelessly vague requests for things like "everything we need to do our jobs." So, Europe decided MVP meant "everything they have today plus any other features they want." North America wanted a whole different set of features.

By contrast, the "right way" to do an MVP is to have very clear objectives. Take the example of Amazon. When it first started out, it was a website selling books. That was really it. That was probably the MVP. Then it started making recommendations on other books you might want, and then it started adding new products to sell. Now on every street in the US and around the globe you see Amazon vans delivering everyone anything they want, ordered up with the touch of a button.

On Project Blast, we were "only" building an MVP, but where Project Ascend wanted us to build every possible feature (a task analogous to trying to launch Amazon.com with every feature it has today), the Project Blast executives knew they had to keep the MVP limited if we were going to launch on time. The best thing we had going for us was that their reputation was also on the line, so they couldn't just keep adding features if they wanted to hit their date.

Our contract had specified a limited set of features and functionality that the MVP needed to include. There were still a lot of details and a design to figure out, but at least we had a box drawn around what we had to do.

The contract specified the high-level features, but we had to make a ton of lower-level decisions as we were designing the website—everything from the look and feel of the website to precisely how all of the features would work.

We had a weekly meeting with the consortium representatives to show them progress, get sign-off on design decisions, and to address any questions we needed to progress.

My team continually wanted to ask the clients what they wanted. It sounds like a reasonable thing, asking. However, there was risk in asking open-ended questions. If their answer specified something too challenging to implement or that would take too long to develop, it would impact our very narrow timeline.

Say for instance I ask, "What do you want for dinner?" You may reply, "Steak!" If I don't have steak, that's going to be a challenge. It's better to ask, "Do you want chicken or pasta?" if I have the ingredients for those meals. Then whichever option you pick is something that can be prepared, and we'll both be happy with dinner.

I told my team that for any design question we needed to offer the client the best solution, which could be completed within the desired timeframe and to confirm it with the clients. Or we would give the client a few options, if they were all equally valid and equally do-able.

As a very simple example, instead of asking, "How do you want this button to work?" We would propose, "The button will be on the bottom of the page, and when you click it, it will open a new page to allow you to choose your options." Telling the client our proposed answer reduced the number of new ideas for harder features that couldn't be built in the timeframe. If they really disagreed with our proposal, we would jointly figure out something that would work for them, but something which was still able to be built in the timeline.

Still, the team continued to want to ask questions. I finally told them, "Every question must be put in the form of a statement." I told them Reverse *Jeopardy!* was our new approach, like the reverse of the popular game show on which every answer had to be put in the form of a question. Reverse *Jeopardy!* was also a specific variation of the Guiding Principle of Critical Thinking, because it forced the team to think through the best possible answer first and then offer it in a statement to the client.

With Reverse *Jeopardy!* as the new philosophy, I finally got the team to start putting out answers for confirmation versus asking open-ended questions that could lead us into trouble with our timeline.

Once I got the team thinking through the answers up front using Reverse *Jeopardy!*, our designs started to take shape and we started to hum on the build. There was still a lot of work to do though, and a lot of things that could go wrong. There was an endless set of challenges that could crop up that we'd have to solve in order to make the five-month (really, three-and-a-half-month) timeline to UAT!

## WHEREVER YOU CAN BEST LEAD

I felt like my job as a leader on Project Blast was keeping one eye on the team to look for any challenge to solve, while also looking ahead to the next phases of work on the horizon, like setting up training and getting ready for operating the website.

It reminded me of another lesson I learned from the military. In the same Army course in which I learned the principle "troops eat first," we also learned how to do patrols. Patrols are when a squad of about eleven soldiers walk through the woods or the jungle to look for and defend against the enemy. Just about every movie on Vietnam shows a squad on patrol.

Our Army instructors told us, "When on patrol, lead the squad from wherever you can best lead."

"What does that mean?" I asked. I wanted more specifics. Did that mean in front? In the middle, or pulling up the rear?

The Army sergeant who was our instructor just repeated himself, "Wherever you can best lead."

Though I was frustrated at first by not getting a clear answer, I think that was an extremely profound point. The leader must be wherever he or she is most needed.

Sometimes, "wherever you can best lead" in a project context meant I needed to decide where to focus. In Project Ascend, that meant that I needed to focus on that terrible root cause analysis (RCA) while my junior leads kept the team moving ahead on our releases.

Other times, "wherever you can best lead" literally means where you can be physically present with your teams. In Project Ascend, my predecessor had squirreled herself away in an office and spent her days on calls and may not even have seen what was happening in the team room. When I took over that project, I picked a desk in the war room where I could see and hear my whole team working. I could overhear people and jump in if they said something that didn't align to a change in direction, and I could see people who were all talk and no action. Being in the middle of the room also made a difference for the team; they saw that I was with them and there for them.

On Project Blast, because we had so little time, we decided we wanted to have as many people working together in person as possible. And because our client was a consortium of clients, it meant we couldn't use their locations like we normally would have.

We managed to reserve space in an office from a company we had recently acquired. We essentially had the run of the place. In addition to the desk space, we had several conference rooms that were almost always free, which was an extremely rare occurrence, especially in New York City. My company's normal New York office was always overbooked and people fought for space. Having that office to ourselves was like walking through Narnia's wardrobe into our own private world.

The same way that people always say that New York City was another character in the show *Sex in the City*, that office became part of the project and part of the success of Project Blast. It was in a beautiful location overlooking St. Patrick's Cathedral on Fifth Avenue, and it was all ours.

I picked a seat facing the other four rows of chairs so that I could oversee and overhear the teams, with the security team next to me. Security was going to be critical for us, so I wanted to keep my focus on that.

After a few weeks, I noticed that our lead security architect was sitting in a different row and would often instant message or email the rest of the security team sitting next to me. There were a few other people who weren't sitting with the people on their specific functional teams, and I could see that it was getting in the way of communication.

I told a few people they had to move and assigned them new seats. I moved the security architect back to my row and aligned all of the cloud architects together. It was much more of a micromanaging move than I had ever made, but I did it. And it worked perfectly. After those few moves, we had one row for security, one row for cloud, and two rows for our functional team. And the energy and the communication level improved across the whole team.

Because that project was so short, I had to stay in control and had to stay one step ahead of the team.

The words of my Army instructors made so much sense in retrospect. It is the job of the leader to decide where to lead from, and how to lead, in order to get the team to where they need to be.

## THE ACCOUNTABILITY AND COMMITMENT TRAP

In order to be "wherever I could best lead" on Project Blast, I'd chosen a desk next to the security team, because cyber security was extremely critical and we would incur a hefty fine if there were any breaches in the platform after it launched.

Most of the team was working together on site in New York, but because of the unique skills required there were a few people who were remote, including a few of the security specialists.

Donna was responsible for one of the layers of security, and Gavin, her manager, was working with her to get her layer aligned with the rest of the plan. The problem was that Donna's work was late. She hadn't provided designs, she hadn't provided the first drafts of the work, and her area was falling behind. And we didn't have a lot of wiggle room for delays.

After Gavin hung up from a conversation with Donna, I asked him what the plan was to recover the time and get the work done. He said Donna had "committed" to have the design work done by the end of the week.

"Gavin, that doesn't make sense," I said. "She had three weeks to do it. Now all of a sudden she can get it done in one week? I don't think she can do it."

He said, "No, she committed to me."

Words like "committed" and "accountability" always send up red flags in my mind and make me stop and find out more. Why? Accountability and commitment are good, right? We want our employees and leaders to be accountable for their work, right? We want employees to commit to getting things done.

Sure, but too often I have seen leaders throwing around phrases like, "I'm holding you accountable," without stopping to ask or understand if the person being held accountable has the right skill and resources, or if there are any challenges holding them back. When leaders use that phrase, "I'm holding you accountable," there often is a subtext of, "You deal with it; I don't want to worry about it."

Similarly, sometimes leaders who say that a worker has committed to them don't necessarily understand what obstacles may be holding that person back from doing the work. Accountability and commitment are two sides of the same coin.

I said, "Gavin, we're not waiting until the end of the week. I need you to see where she is every day, and if she shows you no progress tomorrow, you need to find someone else."

The next day there were more excuses and nothing was getting done. Gavin still wanted to believe that she was going to get the work done, but he agreed that it was time to work another solution. He wasn't an expert in that particular type of security but understood it enough that he started working on the designs himself, and by the end of the week he had a credible start to it.

As expected, Donna had produced nothing. She was rolled off of the project, and I reached out to her supervisor to understand what was going on. That kind of non-performance was really unexpected in my company and perhaps that's why Gavin kept holding on to the belief that she would do the work.

If I had to describe myself as either an optimist or a pessimist, I'd say optimist because I believe that we can achieve things and try to have a positive attitude with the team. But I'm not about to just accept that a glass is half-full and walk away. I'm going to validate that the cup was filled and measure that we received at least a half-full portion, and I'm probably going to inspect the glass to make sure it doesn't have a crack or a hole so the water won't leak out. And I'd want to make sure there was a process to get the glass refilled. Maybe I'm a pragmatist rather than an optimist.

To me, only a true optimist would believe someone who "commits" without stopping to understand if they really are going to be able to do the work.

Similarly, a leader that says, "I'm holding you accountable," doesn't stop to understand if that person has everything they need to accomplish the task at hand. They are essentially saying, "You deal with it; and I'll blame you if you fail."

On Project Triad, Jimmy and the leader that I was replacing both used the language of, "I'm holding you accountable," without stopping to understand what was needed to really make a difference.

When I told Jimmy that the project was structurally unsound and needed to be overhauled, he said he'd agreed to the structure, and we had to make it work. He wasn't going to lose face and say it couldn't be done. Jimmy was "holding me accountable" to make it work and he told the client I was "the accountable executive."

There is a joke I've made about being held accountable. My cat will often push my office door open and wander in when I'm working, forcing me to get up during Teams calls to close the door again. I keep holding my cat accountable for closing the door behind him, but he never does it. Because he's a cat.

Similarly, just saying, "I hold you accountable" may not be enough if there are structural challenges to a project or if the team or leader is lacking certain skills.

Yes, the leader should raise those points if there are challenges, but like the executive who refused to change any of the structural problems of the project—if those points are raised and no action is taken, simply sitting back, pointing a finger, and saying "I hold you accountable" . . . that's not effective, and it's not leadership.

The bottom line is that we needed to get the work done, and accountability and commitment weren't going to be enough to get us there. As always, the focus had to be on solutions. Gavin took the solution from Donna, and we were able to make progress.

## JUST SOLUTIONS

In previous chapters we explored the Guiding Principle, "No Blame; Just Solutions" and how critical it was to both Project Falcon and Project Ascend.

Project Blast was no different. Things went wrong, and my focus and the teams' whole focus had to be on solving whatever came up, like Gavin taking over the security designs when Donna wasn't able to do them.

Perhaps because the timeline was so short, counterintuitively I had to stay calm and take the time to make the right decision. The only thing worse than no decision would have been the wrong decision.

If your team brings you a problem to solve, the first step is to stay calm. You can't come up with creative solutions if you knee-jerk and tell the team to do the first thing that comes to your mind. You can't consider all options necessary to make a decision unless you stay calm.

Most importantly, if you panic, they will panic.

## be calm

On Project Blast, the clients decided that for the beta test they wanted to do a presentation of the new platform in front of an audience of industry executives, and then those same industry people would be able to try out the new platform on about forty laptops we had set up for that purpose.

The fact that we had anything working and ready for the beta date in four and a half months was miraculous, as we had been coming in screeching on every milestone, a hair shy of missing them each time.

The beta industry day was in California, and a few of us flew out to do the demonstration and set up the laptops. My tech team in New York was supposed to be 100 percent focused on care and feeding of the system that day, to make sure it stayed up and running smoothly for the beta day demo and hands-on testing.

We arrived at the auditorium well ahead of schedule and got the demo laptop set up on the podium. We tested the system and it was running smoothly. We tested the projectors and got the forty laptops set up. We had about sixty minutes to spare, and we all held our breath.

About fifteen minutes later, my colleague, Shane, who would be the one to do the actual presentation in front of everyone, sat down next to me in one of the chairs set up for the audience. I had my laptop open and was catching up on a few things. He leaned over to me and whispered, "It's down."

"What did you see?" I asked, hoping to get more clarity. Was it down? Was it just an error message? Was there an issue with the login? What did he see?

"I just tried to get into the system, and it won't load. It's not there."

My heartbeat spiked to 1,000 beats a second. I took a breath and said, "Give me a minute."

I thought I had a good idea of what was happening, but I wasn't sure. I started chatting with my tech team back in New York via instant message. We had several different copies of the system, one for testing, one for development, and one for production. We were using the production copy for the beta testing, which was isolated from the other two. I knew we were doing performance testing on the test and development environments, but there was no way that should affect the production system. They were separated physically.

But it was impacting it. My tech lead confirmed it. Not because of what we built, but because of a downstream system that ours pulled data from. It was getting crushed by all of the performance testing. And both our production and test environments were using the same downstream system, so our beta production site was also getting crushed. The downstream systems were supposed to have different environments for production and testing as well, but for some reason both our production and testing environments were hitting their testing environment.

I stepped out and got my tech lead on the cell phone.

I could have been furious because production was supposed to be 100 percent walled off from the rest of the systems. Performance testing on the lower environments should in no way have impacted production. And because I'd told my team to pamper and baby the system, they should have noticed. But that would not have helped. And the whole reason you do performance testing is to identify those kinds of limitations. But we couldn't have it impact our beta presentation, or we'd be crucified by our clients.

I told them we needed to kill performance testing immediately and get everything back up even faster. The performance testing was shut down, and all of the services were restarted.

About twenty minutes had elapsed at this point, and the early birds were starting to gather in the audience. Shane had turned several shades of green by this point. He said, "We have to tell the clients."

"No, wait. Give me five more minutes." He nodded, but he clearly thought we needed to tell them. He walked away, trying to look natural, greeting some people who were coming in.

Five minutes later, after all of the servers had restarted and the system was reset, my tech lead told me, "Try it now."

I tried, and it loaded.

I walked to Shane and whispered, "It's up."

He very casually walked to the podium laptop, looking like he was just double-checking something, and pulled up the system. It was running, and he was able to run through the full demo.

Beta day went off without a hitch—both with the demo and the industry specialists' hands-on review of the new system.

Shane and I have laughed about that day so many times. He wanted to tell the clients. I knew we needed time to first figure out what the problem was and to potentially solve it. If we had gone running to the clients right away, we would have lost a lot of credibility and worried them unnecessarily. Especially because I knew it was likely a result (Somehow!) of performance testing.

The clients to this day have no idea that there was a glitch because we stayed calm, we thought through the probable causes, and we got the issue resolved quickly.

## if you can't be calm, act calm

It was several years into my tenure as an executive that I got feedback from one of my mentors that I was calm under pressure. I was shocked at first, because I didn't always feel calm. But I got the feedback a few times, and so I started paying attention not only to how I felt but how I came across in pressure-filled situations.

Calm is how I'm feeling when I'm sitting next to a beautiful lake at a sunset with a glass of wine. If Pixar were to animate what's going in my head when the team brings me a problem, it would be a whole team of engineers running up and down stairs and frantically working on blueprints and doing calculations. That's how I feel when a problem comes to me; I'm trying to solve it.

When people tell me I'm calm in the face of problems, I think that it means I don't blame. I ask questions to better understand the issue. I don't immediately react in a knee-jerk way and start giving out orders. I like to have a few possible solutions before acting. I think it's how I respond that makes people say I'm calm.

So, don't worry if you don't *feel* calm; you can still *act* calm with your team. Acting calm with your team is the best way to produce good results and good solutions. If you're freaking out and yelling at your team, they are going to freak out and they may not be able to thoughtfully provide you the best options to go forward.

On Project Blast, I think especially because the timeline was so tight, I had to fight the impulse to make knee-jerk decisions, and being (acting) calm was even more important than normal. Project Blast was a microcosm of team building. We had a tiny timeline to do all of the things necessary to build a great team. We had to get the right people on the team, pushing them to think critically using Reverse

*Jeopardy!*. I had to continually support them through challenges and keep looking ahead to what was coming next.

The most amazing part about Project Blast was not that we accomplished the goals within the timeline. It was that we did it without it being a "death march."

## PROJECT BLAST SUMMARY

Project Blast could have been a total death march. Anything with that tight of a timeline was just made for a 24/7 schedule. But it wasn't.

Yes, we worked hard. Yes, there were long nights. But not every night, and we didn't work weekends.

There were a lot of near misses when things went wrong, or when I didn't think we'd be able to make it work. I put out a status report to my bosses and stakeholders on a weekly basis, sharing the week's accomplishments, the plan for the coming week, and all of the challenges that stood in our way.

There were some challenges I'd never experienced elsewhere that we just had to figure out how to solve. We had a delay getting our Amazon Web Services (AWS) cloud services up because the consortium clients didn't have a payment process yet. My junior leaders had tried to use their American Express (AMEX) cards, but they were rejected. My AMEX had a higher limit (despite what you have heard, they are not limitless), so I threw my card down to pay for the AWS cloud services, a situation that wasn't fully rectified until after the site was live in production. At one point I had $60,000 outstanding on my AMEX.

Of course, there was the near miss at beta testing that almost gave Shane a heart attack.

But it wasn't a death march, in fact it was fun. Why?

We were doing something different, something creative, building something from scratch. That's unusual in our business. On many projects, we're working with software packages or adapting things that already exist. Even if it's a new site you still have to tie into old systems, which create constraints. This was so blue sky, green field, open territory that there was a lot of freedom in it.

It was fun to have most people in the office together—that's unusual these days as well. In many of my past projects, the clients were spread all over, or even if they were in the same building they would often be on calls with each other just to save them the time or the trouble of reserving conference rooms and walking down hallways. I've been on numerous calls when everyone was in the office but no one was together, and that's honestly very frustrating.

On Project Blast we were in it together. The whole team had to work in harmony to make it work.

We established monthly happy hours with the client up front, held on the evening of our monthly status update. It was a great way to build bonds, both with the clients but also across the team.

We met daily as a team to make sure we all knew the progress. If a team was falling behind, we focused on how to solve the issue and what was holding them back. We lived the One Team, and No Blame; Just Solutions philosophies.

Our launch date was a Sunday, simply because that's when the contractual complete-by date of October 1$^{st}$ fell. I decided that there was no need to have the team work the weekend. Wouldn't it be better if we could launch on Friday and then be done and have the weekend clear? I kept telling my team that I wanted our launch day to be so calm, that we could just turn everything up on Friday morning and then eat popcorn and watch a movie in the afternoon.

I didn't think we would really eat popcorn and watch a movie—but this was a brand-new application. We didn't have to convert data from an old system to a new system, like I'd had to do on our three-day Labor Day weekend for Project Falcon. We weren't adding onto an existing system. This launch day should literally be nothing more than making sure the system was "up" and notifying the clients. It was their job to get the users to use the system, and we had an authentication tool set up so that new users would go on and provide their user address and their password.

The point of mentioning popcorn and a movie was to set the expectations, and to make people think through all the steps that would need to be done in order to have the system "available" on Friday morning. The security team provided their steps. The infrastructure team figured out their steps, as did the functional team and operational team.

My job on launch day should simply be to tell the clients that the site was up, so they could start using it.

The morning of the launch, the teams went through all of their steps to bring the site live and make sure everything was connected. We made sure our operations teams were ready to manage the site once it was live. There were a few glitches we had to work through, but then . . . it was done.

I waited until the teams had double-checked that everything was live and working the way it should. It was around 11:00 a.m. that Friday morning.

I filled in the final lines of the emails—and I let them fly.

Our five-month project launched two days early, on a Friday morning.

I told everyone we had a team meeting at noon. There were a few grumbles. It was Friday and the team was exhausted. But I insisted. At noon, I rounded everyone up. "Conference room, now. Let's go."

We had pizza. We had popcorn. And I played a clip of a movie.

The movie was *Guardians of the Galaxy II*. At the beginning of the movie, the Guardians are defending against the attack of a giant many-tentacled squid-like creature. Meanwhile, Baby Groot, the tiny walking tree, is exploring, heedless of the pitched battle ongoing. Various Guardians swooped in and saved Baby Groot and then went back to battling the alien until the alien was vanquished and Baby Groot was safe and still oblivious of the harm he'd been in.

The team laughed and ate their pizza, and then one of my team members asked, "It's great, but why did you choose this clip?"

"The consortium was Baby Groot," I said to the team. "You're the Guardians. You were given a seemingly unbeatable foe—and you fought hard to tackle it, and you did it. The consortium never knew the peril and the risks that the project faced because you did such a good job of both protecting the consortium and defeating the foe. The project was launched, and the consortium's reputation was safe!"

It was exactly the calm and fun launch day that I'd hoped for.

During Project Blast, we had been doing monthly All Hands meetings in New York, and via video for any of the remote teams, including our India team. A few days after launch we had one more scheduled meeting. While I normally had several agenda items to cover in these meetings, to ensure everyone was aware of where we were on the project and what was left, this time I didn't have much content prepared.

I took a few minutes to recap all of my thanks and admiration for the team. I highlighted what a crazy victory it was to launch early in the face of all of the challenges. When I finished, I was ready to end the meeting.

Someone on my team asked if anyone else had anything to add. And then the meeting took on a life of its own. One of the India team members jumped in and basically said it was the best project they'd ever been on.

And then, person by person, the team went around and provided their feedback on the team, echoing the sentiment, until every single person had spoken about how amazing the project was. Their comments filled up and toppled over the hour we'd set aside.

We all knew we'd been part of something special.

What could have been a death march turned into something truly magical.

We had the right people on the team. I had to make some hard choices and roll people off at the beginning to get us there, but it made a difference.

I had to keep pushing the team to Think Critically, using Reverse *Jeopardy!* to keep the scope limited to what we could get done in five months.

And we stayed calm and focused on the solution, focusing on problem solving each time a new issue cropped up that threatened to crush our goals.

But most importantly, we were in it together. We pulled Project Blast out of the hat and got it done.

# 4.

# LEADERSHIP IN LARGE ORGANIZATIONS: PROJECT NEBULA CASE STUDY

The previous Case Studies and chapters have all focused on the team: building teams, supporting teams, managing your people, etc. That is all downward focused leadership. However, leadership is multi-directional.

Unless you're Elon Musk, you will likely have someone you're accountable to. So, in addition to leading your team, you will also have to manage upward, whether that includes your direct bosses or clients, stakeholders from other organizations, or even board members or customers.

What is managing up? Managing up is the set of actions you must accomplish with your bosses or stakeholders, including such activities as communicating status and progress, requesting help, representing members of your team in feedback and promotion discussions, and giving and taking credit for the success (or failure) of the project.

Managing up can sometimes be thought of negatively. When people are talked about as being "good at managing up," there can be an implication that they spend more time working the politics and taking credit for their team's actions, and not focusing on or leading the team.

In some cases that may be true. But there is a middle ground, where the best leaders both manage upward, and continue to lead and support their team as needed. Just as there are negative implications for primarily managing up, there are also negative consequences if a leader *only* focuses on the team and doesn't focus enough on the senior leadership.

I'll address implications for both upward management and downward leadership, as I think there are critical nuances of each.

## chain of command versus matrixed organization

How you will need to manage up will depend on how your organization is structured.

The military, and many of the companies I worked with across various industries are hierarchical and everyone falls into a very specific chain of command, which includes the leader directly over you and their direct leaders up the chain of leadership.

In hierarchical organizations, managing up can be very straightforward, with everything having to flow through your direct boss. However, even in those kinds of organizations there are other stakeholders that may need to be informed of your team's work.

There are also implications for promotions, as to get to the next level you may need your name and your reputation to be known above that direct-boss level, or you may need approvals or decisions from above your boss's level. Working with that direct boss may be the best way to get what you need without "jumping the chain of command," but you still need to be aware of what other levels or stakeholders need to be involved in decisions and ratings.

Many other organizations are in a matrixed organizational structure where you may be reporting to multiple organizations, and you may need to make sure that each of those bosses is aware of your performance, or, you may need to approach each of them for various kinds of help, approvals, or decisions.

The consulting firm I worked in is a matrixed organization and has a regional boss, plus the boss of the project or the account you're on, plus the leader of the practice your headcount is assigned to. Oftentimes, I felt like there were five to ten people who might say "jump" and I'd have to hop to.

Over twenty-five years, I worked at multiple client companies and served as a quality reviewer for several others, so I gained awareness of how many other companies operated. Even for those "hierarchical" organizations, there was still a lot of collaboration between units, especially between business units and IT or network units that had to come together to get various projects done. An employee in one of those organizations might need to work across those various units, not just up through their boss.

Understanding how your organization is structured, and who the stakeholders are for your work, both in support of your team's objectives and performance, is critical to your success and to the success of the project.

Project Nebula was a major initiative to transition a product from being on server-based hardware to being modular and dynamic. It was going to be a massive transformation; a multi-year, multimillion-dollar program.

The company where Project Nebula was being implemented was a matrixed organization with numerous key stakeholders. Bill was the business stakeholder responsible for the funding and rollout of the new technology. His counterpart, Steve, was the technical mastermind behind it. Steve's team had just implemented a prototype to make sure the product would work on it.

It was earlier in my career, and I had not yet reached the executive level. I was on a contract to Bill, who could leverage me to do any work in his department. By then, I had been working with him for about two years and had completed multiple projects for him, and I had earned his trust. I'll provide more about that in the upcoming sections.

Bill told me, "Go get involved in Project Nebula."

At the time I knew nothing about the project or the technology behind it, and I had no authority besides working on Bill's behalf "to get involved." I essentially operated as an employee of Bill's company, but I wasn't one. I didn't have direct authority over anyone except one team member who was also on my contract with Bill.

That project taught me a lot about managing in a matrixed company and leadership by influence, and I got a front seat view to what Bill had to do to manage the politics of his company.

Bill was a master at leading by influence because he had very little direct authority either. I had to figure out how to navigate the company in order to drive Project Nebula. Because, let's face it, he didn't want me to "get involved," he wanted me to lead it; he just couldn't tell me to lead it because he didn't have that authority either.

In the matrixed organization where we had no real authority, it became clear very quickly how important relationships were, as well as the flip side of relationships: dealing with difficult people. I'll also cover communications and asking for help, which were also critical. I'll use Project Nebula as a reference through this section but will also refer back to a few more examples from Projects Blast, Ascend, and Falcon.

# RELATIONSHIPS

Building strong relationships is vital to being able to lead and build a strong team. Why? Can't the leader just march in and tell everyone what to do? No, even in the military, as I saw from my very first days as a young lieutenant, I couldn't pretend to be General Patton and shout out orders.

Even in the military, I had to make relationships and lead by influence.

In the civilian world, and especially in a highly matrixed organization, leadership is all about influence. And influence relies on relationships. Leadership is all about relationships, both up the chain and with the team.

There are a couple of key points that I learned regarding both downward and upward relationships.

## respect before relationships

All of the principles we've been talking about throughout the other case studies, including listening to your team, supporting your team ("troops eat first"), not blaming your team, and providing the right structure for your team—all of those principles help a leader build a strong relationship with the team.

But is that enough, or do you need to build strong bonds with individuals on the team as well? Is building individual relationships necessary for the team to feel like a family? One of my mentors used to say that he knew a team was gelled when team members knew the names of each other's kids and dogs. One of my peers excelled at knowing all of her people; she knew their names, and their interests, their families seemingly the instant she walked into a team.

I found that I needed to understand the team members, their capabilities, and how they fit into the overall team before I could begin to get close to anyone. As the leader, I was responsible for both the overall team success and people's individual performance ratings. Which meant that I would need to decide on performance ratings at the end of the year, and I may need to roll some people off if their performance wasn't in line with what the team needed.

To me, it was too risky to be friendly with someone until I respected them and knew how they were going to fit into the team. The only thing worse than having to roll off a friend was keeping that friend on the team if they were not performing well.

Nothing could impact a team worse than a leader praising or ignoring the poor performance of a "friend" who isn't pulling their weight on the team, or being more friendly with one person, leaving others of similar performance to feel like they're not going to be treated fairly. Leaders must be careful to not be biased or even appear biased.

For me, only after I respected someone's capabilities and knew how they were contributing to the team, could I start to build a relationship with them as a person. And I would try to build relationships with individuals across the team so that people wouldn't feel like I was being biased.

I would often build a strong personal relationship with the next level down, my junior leaders, but I would try to build a strong relationship with all of them equally. I'm positive I was never entirely unbiased, but I did my best to be.

If there is such a risk of potential bias, is it worth building strong individual relationships with people on your team? What's the advantage?

I have found that making strong relationships with that next layer of leadership leads to a deeper level of trust. The more I know them, the more I trust them to do the right thing, and the more they trust that I'm doing what's in the team's and their best interest. The deep trust helps the team function without friction, and helps the team feel more like a family. The tighter the relationships, the deeper the trust.

A friend of mine who works in the media industry found herself in a leadership role for the first time and told me how true she found my advice. Unfortunately, she learned the hard way. She had gotten friendly with one of the people on the team immediately and then found herself regretting it when the person turned out to not be as capable as needed, and my friend was going to have to take action.

## downward: leading by influence

Bill hadn't explicitly told me to take over or lead Project Nebula, he just told me to "get involved." So, I had no real authority, though people knew I worked for Bill, which gave me some credibility.

To understand the program and build a program plan, I had to build a relationship with all of the key leads on the project and earn their trust.

The team was organized in a "flat structure," with everyone having a voice and a role. I wasn't in charge, and frankly neither was Bill. No one on the program team worked directly for Bill because of the matrixed structure of the company. Bill owned the budget. Steve was the technical lead, but he was in a different organization in the company.

Though it may seem counterintuitive, my military experience came in very handy in Project Nebula. The same way I would have lost credibility as a twenty-one-year-old lieutenant with no experience in the missile fields of North Dakota if I had tried to beat on my chest and tell everyone I was in charge, I had no authority to step into Project Nebula and tell everyone what to do. I didn't push my way in and say I was the boss. That might work for some, but in this context, when I was not an employee (though I was operating as one), and it being a matrixed company, that wasn't going to earn me any respect.

Instead, I focused on listening and understanding everything that needed to be done to get this technology set up. I started with the lead architect and asked a ton of questions to build the picture and the plan, asking questions based on the learnings from the two previous years I'd worked with Bill. After meeting the lead architect, I met with each of the project's individual engineers, who came from different organizations and even different companies.

It was very much a case of the blind men and the elephants, where every engineer I talked to described only their individual responsibility, like explaining how Project Nebula was long and thin like a trunk, or fat and broad like the sides of the elephant. No one, not even the lead architect, knew the full picture. Valuing their individual contributions and being able to take all of the disparate information and fit it into an overall plan, made people respect what I was doing for the program and want to listen to me.

Based on the plan I'd cobbled together with everyone's input, I started running weekly meetings to make sure that everyone was on track with their pieces of the work. It was a collaborative session, not just a status read-out. I met with everyone individually for five minutes ahead of time, so that during the meeting I could prompt people to highlight the things that could impact the other teams around the table. The others around the table also asked questions, because everyone needed to understand how the elephant was being built up.

I established an attitude of trust in the meetings, which, given the fact that there were multiple organizations from the client company, plus multiple software and hardware vendors, it could have been extremely contentious.

It was an oddly structured program, when I look back at it. So many different vendors, with me plopped into an organizational role in the middle without explicit authority. But it worked because of the relationships and the trust that had been built up. Everyone felt my focus was on the success of the project, not on trying to expand my consulting company's revenue or make the other vendors look bad.

to contrast . . .

On Project Triad, the clients kept assuming that we had done programs like theirs "all the time," which isn't remotely true. Building four different systems with three competing vendors owning different slices of the program pie wasn't remotely "normal." I'd only seen programs with two or three vendors be successful if each vendor took one of the systems and did it end to end, versus trying to divvy up the systems by phase. To go back to my house analogy, it might have been successful if ACME Contracting had done everything on the kitchen from design to build, while Joe's Contracting did the same for one bathroom, and the third company did the same on a different bathroom. There would still need to be some coordination, but it would be a lot more successful than the scenario where ACME did the designs for all of the rooms, and the other two companies did the remodel work on them.

I thought back to anything I'd done in my career that could inform how best to manage Triad, and I thought back to Program Nebula. It was similar in terms of the multiple vendors involved, as well as involvement from different organizations of the client company.

One of the major factors that made Project Nebula successful was that we had strong relationships across all of the vendors and created a collaborative environment.

In Project Triad my company had been acting as if we were primary and treating the other vendors as subordinate to us, except they were on their own contracts and we had no authority over them. We were holding them at arm's length and not treating them as full collaborators. We always produced our schedules or plans and first reviewed them among our own company, then sometimes with the client, then would eventually pass it to the other vendors. Obviously, this caused a rift with the other vendors, and they complained about us to the client and stated that we weren't collaborating with them (and they were right!).

One of the first things I did (in addition to trying to repair the relationship rifts within my own team and listening to them) was to start building relationships with the other vendors. If we were going to succeed in the project, we had to succeed together. We would have to do the strategy and design well, and we would have to make sure they were in agreement with the design and ready to build it.

I met the leads of the other companies and set up a regular cadence with them. I listened to some of the challenges they'd been experiencing with the project. We started to turn the ship around, going from us leading with two other partners being towed behind us, which made none of us happy, to having all three in the same boat and rowing in the same direction.

But, as I've mentioned in previous chapters, the project was too far gone before I came in. The other vendors were working behind our backs to take over more of the work.

Some might say that these competing vendors would never have played the game fairly and were always going to work behind our backs to take more work. Maybe that's true. But I believe that if the project had been structured fairly and relationships built from the start we would have been in a much better position than where we ended up.

Relationships, within the whole ecosystem you're working in, are critical to the success of a program.

## upward: relationships with bosses and stakeholders

Why is it important for a leader to make a good relationship with his/her boss, clients, or stakeholders?

Going back to "troops eat first," one of the most important roles of a leader is to protect his/her team and provide air cover when needed. Without good relationships with leadership, you can't protect your team. Good relationships allow a leader to negotiate good contracts or to push back on overly aggressive timelines or to align on mutually beneficial goals. If the leader doesn't have a good relationship with the boss or the client, the team may suffer.

That was the situation in the Project Ascend team when I walked in. The leader was sitting down in the war room firing off escalation notes, which just doubled the pressure on the team. But she never walked upstairs to the CIO's office, never built a relationship with the right people in the company. The first week I was there I told the CIO I needed to meet with him at least once a week, and he said I'd already been in his office more than my predecessor had ever been. The team suffered because she had no relationship with the client leadership.

How does one go about building a strong relationship with one's boss or client? How do you build relationships with other leaders?

There are several principles that I have found most useful over the years, and which have allowed me to build strong relationships with most of my clients. We'll cover more on what to do when it's a struggle to build a relationship in "Dealing with Difficult People," the next section in this chapter.

## do the job

Your boss or stakeholder is likely also a leader, which means their job is also to build a team to get objectives accomplished. This is true whether you are building a consulting team or a team within a company. You are one of the players on their chess board that they're using to get the job done. So the most important thing you can do to build a strong relationship with your boss or client is to do a great job for them.

I started working with Bill on Project Nebula right after getting promoted to senior manager, the leadership position right before the executive level. The role was supposed to be building out business requirements for a new product, something I had experience in, and which I thought would be helpful for my career.

When I got on site, Bill said, "No, we're not ready for that. I need you to go clean up our process for rolling out new territories." I was essentially on contract to Bill to be a member of his staff, so he could leverage me however he wanted. The role he was asking me to do was so far under my skill level, I felt like it was one step above asking me to get coffee for everyone. I was a senior manager, and he wanted me to clean up a rollout process? I gritted my teeth and jumped in, figuring out what the problems were, figuring out who the key players were, and building relationships with them. About two months later, the job was running smoothly and Bill handed me the next project, a definitive step up in terms of responsibility.

After I'd finished two other projects for him, I'd earned Bill's trust. I was essentially working directly for him, operating as an employee rather than a consultant, because he knew he could trust me both to get the job done and to keep him informed. Bill and I worked together for five years.

Contrast the trust I'd built with Bill, having proved I could make him successful, with a salesperson in my company named Adam, who I was mentoring. Adam was trying to figure out how to build a relationship with his boss and failing. He wanted to invite his boss out to lunch. I knew his boss and knew his boss's opinion of Adam. The boss believed that Adam had a lot of good ideas but he just didn't generate enough sales. Either he spent too much time on "good ideas" that didn't pan out, or he spent too much time doing other things. He needed to focus on getting the job done (closing deals, in his case) in order to build respect and a relationship with his boss. His boss, just like me, couldn't be friendly with or trust someone who wasn't able to get the job done. Adam was a chess piece on the boss's team, but he was so focused on building a relationship he wasn't making the right moves.

## have their interests at heart

Steve didn't like consultants. You may recall he was the technical lead on Project Nebula, so I had to work with him as closely as I did with Bill, possibly closer. Steve was the brains behind the operation, Bill owned the budget, and my job was executing Steve's vision and product within Bill's budget.

After Bill told me to get involved, I met with Steve several times to understand Project Nebula and start developing the framework to organize it, before he realized I was a consultant.

I didn't introduce myself as anything other than working for Bill, and so Steve assumed I was an employee of their company. By the time he figured it out, he had already accepted me and I was "in" with him because he knew I was working for the good of his company and for him.

My job was to make Project Nebula successful, which would also make both Steve and Bill successful, and Steve trusted me. He and I worked hand in hand for years and I could walk into his office at any time because he trusted me to do the right thing for him and the company.

## critical thinking: address the intent

Our bosses or clients rely on us not just to do the job they tell us to do, but to bring our own critical thinking to the challenge. Critical thinking is one of my key guiding principles for a reason. If our bosses and stakeholders wanted people who would do exactly as they were told, they could get junior resources who would do what they were told for a lot less money.

One of my clients, Rebecca, was initially very challenging to work with. Rebecca was extremely smart and had a very good radar for upcoming risks. When she sensed a risk, she would tell me what to do about it in a tone that allowed no argument. But I was closer to the details, so while I agreed that she was right about the risk, I didn't always agree with her solution to it. Arguing was useless. The more I tried to push my point, the more she would fight back. But I knew the solution she wanted me to pursue was wrong.

She, like many bosses, didn't like to be argued with or countermanded. I bristled and fought back against her leadership until I figured out the best way to work with her. I learned to listen to her directive and just nod my head. But an hour or a day later, I could go back to her with, "I've been thinking about what you asked me to do, and here's another approach that I think might work." When I didn't directly confront her and gave her space, and when I gave myself time to think about the right solution, then we had some great discussions and she often did agree with my adjustment. Sometimes there was another factor that I wasn't aware of which made her solution better.

Rebecca worked for Bill, so I would get direction from her on Project Nebula as well. Right after I got involved in Project Nebula, when I was still trying to understand what we were going to have to do to make the technology scale from the prototype, Rebecca told me to start working on the deployment plan. I had done a deployment plan for a previous product, and I knew what she was looking for—a very detailed step-by-step plan by which the technology would be enabled across the country.

She was right that we needed to know how the solution was going to be deployed, but we just weren't there yet. It was like someone telling a general contractor that they needed to figure out the color scheme for each room when the blueprint wasn't even finished, and the concrete hadn't been poured on the foundation. I knew if I started asking the engineers the equivalent of the color schemes of the rooms at this early stage, they'd look at me like I was crazy. I nodded my head, and said we'd work on it, knowing that if I said no, she'd just push and push and push until I said yes.

I started thinking about why she would be asking for this now . . . she knew as well as I did that it was extremely early in the process. As I thought about it, I realized she was uncomfortable that we didn't know what it would take to get this product out to the field. She was addressing her discomfort with her statement to build a deployment plan.

Steve's team that had prototyped the new technology was an extremely smart set of technical engineers. The program plan I'd built based on all of their input included all of the steps it would take to set up a production-level version of the technology they'd prototyped. But would that be enough? Was there anything left to do after it was in production?

I went to the lead engineer and asked, "Once the product is up, then what?"

The engineer said, "Then nothing. Getting the system up is the plan. That's the focus. It's a national system. It will serve everywhere; we just need to stand it up."

"Great," I said. "So, as soon as it's up, a customer in Connecticut will just automatically be using the service?"

The engineer paused, finally hearing me. He thought about it and finally answered, "Ummmmmm . . . no."

"Ok, so . . . how does the customer in Connecticut start using it?"

That was the key question that my client knew the engineers hadn't solved (and hadn't even realized there was a question). Getting the equipment up was no small task, but it was only the first step in a much more complex effort to get the product available to every region.

Once again, I had to meet with every single engineer on the project and interview them to get them to think about the steps that would be needed to get their piece of the puzzle to be used everywhere. Then, we had to build a plan to get that done. It was again like the old man and the elephants, and it felt like we had to understand each person's perspective and then built it together to get the full vision of what it would take to get the product to each region.

Rebecca was right that they didn't know what it was going to take to deploy the product, and she was absolutely right to be worried that the engineers didn't know. It wasn't the right time to draw up the colors by room, but . . . because I had understood what her real concern was, I was able to tell her how we were going to work with the engineers to come up with a blueprint (a higher level set of steps that would be implemented during the build), which would be the first step to get us to that deployment plan. Her intuition of the risk was critical for us to start drawing out the path for deploying the product once the solution was up.

Once I figured out to listen first, think second, and then propose an alternate if needed, we got along great. She trusted me to do the right thing, and trusted that I was bringing my own point of view to the solution.

## know what each person needs and adapt accordingly

At Project Nebula, I worked with a very wide span of clients and vendors to get the work done. I had been at the client company for years and had known many of these leaders for a long time. Depending on who I was writing an email to, the email would often sound very different; the "voice" changing dramatically based on my audience. One leader from Denver was extremely plain-spoken, a veteran like me, and the "voice" I would use for him would be friendly and open. But when I wrote to some of the executives at headquarters, the tone would be professional and tight, the email taking no more than three lines.

Is that being an "authentic" leader? Shouldn't I just be me in each of these emails? Can't my singular, authentic voice be used everywhere? I think one of the most overused words in the sphere of leadership books is "authentic." It is one of those words that will make me roll my eyes every time.

When it comes to communicating with anyone, whether they are your bosses or your team members, you need to communicate to your audience. You need to speak or write *to them*, in the way that they are most likely going to understand. To do that you need to adapt to them.

Some of my clients think and make decisions with numbers, so I needed to give them numbers. Some people operated much more based on gut-level intuition, so I needed to tell them all of the risk factors they should take into account. Some people were friendlier and preferred a few friendly phrases as an opener. That's not inauthentic;

that's respect for who you're working with. That's understanding who people are. That's working with people as human beings not as roles. That's what it takes to build relationships with each individual.

The best example I have of adapting to individual leaders is the time I had to get the customer support vice president, Jake, engaged in Project Nebula. As the project got nearer to rollout, I called Jake and told him I was coming out to Denver and wanted to meet with him so that I could explain how his organization would need to be involved. Jake said that he wanted to see me, plus the technical lead, Steve, and the project manager. We were to meet in his office at 6:00 a.m. (seriously, 6:00 a.m.). When Steve and I arrived to meet with Jake, he asked me to draw out the architecture of the product we were deploying in Project Nebula.

Steve was there, but he didn't say anything. Jake had clearly addressed the question to me. This was a test.

Jake knew I was a consultant and was distrustful of me because of it. (Distrust of consultants was common in that client company.) I had no problem drawing out the architecture. I'd had to understand it to build out the program plan and to manage the overall program. In fact, I probably understood the end to end, including the IT systems, even better than Steve. I had finished drawing out the architecture and addressing all Jake's myriad of questions, when the client project manager finally showed up thirty minutes late. Jake turned the paper over and asked her to explain the architecture on the blank side. She couldn't. Even worse, she tried to say that she didn't need to know it. At that point, she was basically dead to the VP and he would never listen to her again.

From that point on, whenever I needed to meet with Jake I always met with him at 6:00 a.m., and I always came prepared with the technical basis behind the work that I needed him to do for the program. I was always the interface to him, never the project manager. That's what he wanted; that's how he worked. I had to respond accordingly.

## meet them in person

If I had not been willing to fly to Denver to meet with Jake (and go to his office at 6:00 a.m.!), I would never have built the relationship I had with him. I couldn't as easily have conveyed both my willingness to do whatever was needed for the program, but also my knowledge of the program, without being there in person. We were able to work through a lot of challenges because I'd established that trust early on.

I'll cover more about meeting people in person in the "Remote Work" section of the book.

## read the room

The same way you must adjust to individual client or bosses' personalities, you may also have to adjust your day-to-day approach based on their mood, their time, or their attention. To do that, you need to be able to read the room and understand if you need to shift.

For example, Steve was very smart and understood concepts quickly. As soon as he understood something, he was done with the conversation and ready to move on. As soon as I saw that he got it, I would stand up and get ready to depart, even if I was in mid-sentence. If I had my junior leader with me, sometimes I would all but elbow him in the ribs to get him to move because he hadn't seen the same signal and would keep making his point.

I also had a client who had a Jekyll and Hyde temperament and could shift back and forth multiple times during the day. We often asked whether "Good Jack" or "Bad Jack" was in the meeting, because you never knew which one you would get.

You had to go in prepared for Bad Jack, and if you got Good Jack then you could lighten up the mood and make small talk and bring up more contentious topics. If it was Bad Jack, you needed to "read" that in the room, say as little as possible, and try to get out of the meeting as quick as possible.

## set up one-on-ones

I found that setting up recurring one-on-one meetings with my stakeholders or bosses when we began working together was critical for relationship-building. A recurring meeting from the beginning allowed us to discuss expectations or catch up on how things were going before we started hitting challenges. A recurring one-on-one allowed both the positive and negative to be discussed from the outset.

If that recurring time isn't established, the likely scenario is that the client or the boss will be getting calls only when issues or emergencies are happening. Which means that every call they get from you will be associated with the negative. Having an ongoing one-on-one enabled me to establish a sound relationship before stuff started hitting the fan, as it inevitably does.

It's also more respectful of your stakeholders' time. I had one peer who liked to tout the philosophy of "management by walking around" and would wander to the clients' offices with a cup of coffee and stick his head in their doors. The problem with that is that the clients had things they were trying to get done or they were in the middle of meetings, so his efforts were of limited effectiveness. I rolled him off the project shortly after I took over because I didn't find his style of management particularly useful. If you can't get a recurring meeting because their calendar is packed, then work with your boss or client, or their Executive Assistant if applicable, to get frequent checkpoints on the calendar. The crucial point is to meet and build the relationship before the issues begin.

Building relationships is hard work, and relationships need constant maintenance. You can't just show up whenever it's convenient to you or you'll lose credibility.

One client I worked with, Tina, refused to meet with my boss because "he only came around when there was a possible sale." She and I had worked together and had met many times. I mentored her when she was trying to get promoted in her company, and we talked about family and balance (or lack thereof). I could always get her ear and on her calendar. My boss had proven time and again that he had no time for her unless it benefitted him. She wouldn't meet with him.

And some people are more difficult to build relationships with than others. In fact, there are some people I just could never build a relationship with. We were wired differently.

To me, they were difficult people. There are ways of dealing with difficult people, but sometimes you just may not be able to build a strong relationship.

## DEALING WITH DIFFICULT PEOPLE

Difficult people are just those individuals you don't have a good relationship with.

I've had a lot of clients that others found "difficult," but I had a good relationship with them, so they were never "difficult" with me. There have also been people that I found terribly difficult that others managed to work with perfectly fine.

As an example, I got along well with one of my key clients at a Mega Program called Hydra (more on that program later). She and I worked through many tricky situations together, and we built up trust with each other. One of my bosses wanted to meet with her, so I set up a three-way meeting at his request.

He didn't come in person when he'd said he would. Then he was late to the call. When he joined, he used a lot of examples that weren't relevant to her area, and he didn't seem to really understand where she fit in the organization. He hadn't prepared for the meeting well, if at all. He had underestimated her, and she was not impressed. She was an extremely influential member of her organization and one whisper from her could sway the bosses. My boss always considered her "difficult" after that, but I think she just didn't suffer fools. He had acted foolishly by underestimating her and under-preparing for the meeting.

If you're struggling with someone you consider difficult, try to build a relationship with them. Go back to the last section and see if there are some principles there that might apply.

But also, know that you won't always be able to build a great relationship with everyone. Sometimes people are just oil to your water, and you may need to come up with a different strategy to work with or around them.

I've included a few examples of challenging people with whom I had to figure out how to build a relationship, as well as some strategies for working with people with whom you don't have a good relationship.

If your normal way of working isn't resulting in a good relationship with someone, you either have to adjust your style (go back to the principles in the "Relationships" section), or recognize that you're just not going to be able to build a relationship with that person.

## personnel challenges

There is a difference between being "difficult," which in my mind is just being challenging to work with but still within the bounds of professionalism. And there are people that cross from being difficult into an unacceptable level of inappropriateness or bullying.

If someone is acting in an inappropriate manner, it is necessary for a leader to take action. Below are a couple of examples of when people's actions crossed the line, moving from "difficult" to creating situations that Human Resources (HR) might need to address.

**Inappropriate jokes.** On one of my recovery projects, a young client was getting too personal with the team and making inappropriate jokes. For example, he once came into a meeting and all of the seats were full. He joked that he could just sit in one of the young women's laps. Yikes! Several of the young women raised his behavior to me and told me they were very uncomfortable around him. I had not personally witnessed the behavior or I would have addressed it earlier. As soon as the young women raised it to me, I knew I had to act.

I could have just raised it to the leaders on the client side, and let them deal with it and take it to HR if needed. But this client was also one of our better clients in terms of supporting us and helping us get problems resolved, so I wanted to see if I could correct the behavior by talking to him.

I let his boss know that we'd seen some issues, and that I wanted to talk to him first before any further action was taken. The boss agreed, so I met with the client one-on-one.

I thanked him for all of his help with the team and told him that I thought he had a lot of potential in his company. Then I let him know that some of his comments were not appreciated and were not appropriate in the workplace. He was honestly surprised and had really thought he was just building relationships. I gave him a few of the examples of when his jokes had crossed the line and the way those actions were perceived. He thanked me for the input, and we never had a problem with him again.

The women thanked me for handling the situation, and there was an immediate boost to morale because it had been addressed.

**Abusive language.** On a different project, there was a woman from our consulting firm who was part of a different workstream. She was junior to me, but she didn't report to me. She decided that a few people on the technology team were no good, and she demanded that I roll them off. The individuals in question didn't work for her, though they interacted with her because their technology work connected to her workstream.

I listened to her feedback, then I met with the individuals to get an understanding of their side of the story and I gave them some coaching. The individuals had very specific skillsets and the clients thought they were doing a good job, so I wasn't about to roll them off just because one person on a totally different workstream team said so.

When I didn't roll them off, she started bullying me, my team, and those individuals. She said we were wasting the client's money by keeping them on the program. Because of how that program was structured, she was in a different group, and I didn't have the authority to roll her off.

I told my boss about it, as she and I both reported to him. He said he'd talk to her. I think he did, but it had no effect. She was more brutal than ever. She would message me horrible things, calling me names and telling me no one likes me and that the boss had made a mistake bringing me on. Once, after we were all on a team meeting together where she appeared perfectly reasonable and calm in front of our boss, she called me directly afterward and screamed at me for ten minutes about how I was doing everything all wrong. I tried to be professional, maintained my calm, and used pacifying language like, "I hear you; I will look at it. I understand your point of view." But none of that changed her behavior.

After that episode, I called the boss again. I was upset and he knew it. But he said he didn't want to roll her off because there was a big sale pending, reliant on her being part of the team. He basically said, he'd try to calm her down, but to just deal with it.

That was not acceptable, and I couldn't believe he wasn't willing to stand up and do what was right for his team. I would never ask anyone on my team to just deal with that kind of abuse.

Eventually, the client cut the portion of the program that this woman was leading, so she rolled off along with her team. My technology team continued forward.

## relationships with stakeholders and bosses

**The don't-argue-with-me types.** In the Relationships section, I highlighted Rebecca, who worked for Bill on the Nebula project, because we eventually established a very solid relationship that endured years. But working with her for the first couple of months was challenging. She would tell me what to do, and saw any discussion as arguing, which only made her dig in. I was so frustrated until I figured out how to work with her, which was never to confront her head-on, but to come back with suggestions later if needed.

I later had another client my team considered to be a bully, but I was always able to work with him because I knew not to confront him head-on, and I was never afraid of him. If I disagreed with the approach he presented my team, I would come around to the side with a, "Here's another approach I've seen work," kind of dialogue, and he was generally open to discuss it with me.

My advice is that if you push directly back, you may find yourself head-to-head with a Mack truck. If you step aside and come around with another option, someone is more likely to listen.

**The "Involve me" micromanagement type.** I'm a get-it-done type, and I operate best when I'm in an environment where I have autonomy. I had one client who wanted to be involved and have her fingerprints on the work. She didn't go so far as micromanaging, but I had to remember to involve her and run things past her more often. As soon as I would forget and get too focused, she'd get frustrated with me again. I had to figure out the right cadence with her so that she felt involved enough, without it taking so much time that I wasn't getting the work done.

As I had to with this manager, with most of your bosses you'll need to determine the right amount of updating and involvement they prefer. And there could be some friction if your boss wants more frequent updates, especially if it veers into micromanagement.

**The IKEA effect.**[2] The IKEA effect essentially says that if you put in the hard work to build something, you will like it more than something ready-made. Even if your IKEA bookcase is slightly lopsided because you missed a screw somewhere, you'll like it better than the perfectly straight one delivered to your door. I have found this to be true in a team setting as well.

One of our clients always seemed to favor one of the competitor teams even though they were continually having issues. I couldn't understand why our client continued to favor them until he told the story of how he had spent long hours and nights helping them integrate into his company and how they'd been so messed up at the beginning that he'd had to jump in to make it work. He favored them because he had poured so much attention and work into that team. And no matter that they were still lopsided, he was always going to have a soft spot for them.

I think the best way to navigate this one would be to get the client or boss involved and bring them in to "solve" a problem that you're having. Even if you have to manufacture a problem or expose a problem you might not ordinarily want to. The more he or she jumps in to "help" you, the more he or she might start developing the same soft spot for your team.

**Annoying people.** There are a wide range of people who you will have to work with whom you will consider annoying. They may ask status of you three times a day or they may not be very competent. (I had one client who used a calculator to incorrectly add up all of the cells in the Excel sheet, before proceeding to ask us why the data was wrong.) They may be perpetually glass-half-empty people and always complaining about the rain.

My advice for dealing with any of these types is, if they are not directly under your control and you can't take any actions, use what I call the "quirky family member philosophy." In every family there is usually one person who is quirky. It does me no good to be upset or frustrated by that person; they're part of the family. They're not going away and they're not going to change. Similarly, there's no point in doing anything with some of these "annoying" people, other than tolerating them and supporting them with patience and grace.

**Kiss-the-ring types.** My client on Project Falcon was the one who didn't show up during our three-day Labor Day deployment, and he'd still had the nerve to call it "good leadership" when he showed up in the office Tuesday morning.

My typical approach of working hard and doing a good job didn't work for him. He liked my team; he just never liked me.

My boss came in and met with him and told me that this client is a "kiss-the-ring type." He wants to be revered, honored, and told how smart he is. He wants someone to come in and kiss the ring whenever they meet with him. That was the first time I'd encountered someone like that, and I would never have understood him without my boss's comments. When he said it, it all made sense and it rang true.

There was no way I would call him a good leader and tell him how smart he was. And even if I could force myself to do it, "You're a *$%!" still would be written all over my face and he'd know I wasn't sincere. There's no way I could compliment him sincerely. My boss, however, was a natural at it. He had no problem kissing the ring. While some of my other clients didn't like my boss because they thought he came across as insincere, for this client he was ideal. Anything I needed to convey to this client, from then on I deferred to my boss, and I limited my interactions with the client to saying hello in the hallway.

Bottom line, if you can "kiss the ring" and create a strong relationship with someone like that, do it. If you can't, like I couldn't, then see if there is someone else on your team who can do it for you.

## INTENTIONAL COMMUNICATIONS

In order to maintain good relationships with both your team and your stakeholders, you need to keep them informed and make sure they are aware of everything that could impact them. But . . . do you need to tell them everything? Can you maintain a good relationship and hold things back from them?

I don't believe you need to tell everyone everything. There are times to hold back for the sake of your team, your project, or the companies involved.

Just like "authenticity," "transparency" is one of those words that we use all of the time and never stop to really think about the meaning. There seems to be a belief that transparency is the pinnacle of communication, that the more transparency the better, and that transparency fosters team engagement and better relationships.

I would advocate intentional communications over full transparency.

Whether you are communicating to your team or upward to your leadership or stakeholders makes a difference in what you choose to communicate. It's good to consider several questions before sharing, such as: How will the information impact the company? How will the team morale be impacted? Will an individual's performance or career be benefitted or harmed by the information?

## upward communications: when action is needed

Action is needed from a boss or stakeholder in situations when a decision needs to be made, such as when additional funding is needed, when a change in timeline is likely, when there is a need for additional resources, and so on. Whenever there are actions needed from stakeholders, it's best to communicate as early and as often as possible.

For example, as painful as it can be to admit when the team is behind on the timeline and won't achieve the date for whatever reason, the issue needs to be raised and discussed as early as possible so that new schedules can be determined. There have been countless times over my career when the schedule just couldn't be hit. And regardless of where the issues arose, or who would blame whom, the schedule had to be changed; action needed to be taken.

One of my mentor's favorite expressions is "bad news doesn't age well." If there is bad news to discuss, bad news that requires action, like a change in schedule, face the discussion as early as possible. The only thing worse than having the discussion is waiting and hoping the issue will go away, only later to have the boss or client figure it out and get even angrier that the problem hadn't been raised as soon as it was discovered.

Whatever the reason, if action needs to be taken, the stakeholders need to be told as soon as possible.

## upward communications: when there is nothing actionable

On the other hand, if there are no actions needed, sometimes it may be better to hold back.

We knew that Project Blast was risky right out of the gates, but we'd agreed to do it, and we had a plan we thought could work. But it was so risky that on week one we debated whether we should show the status as red or green to the clients.

Different people use the classic red, yellow, and green statuses differently depending on the culture and company. In my mind, green means we're on track according to the plan. Yellow means there is a risk to the plan, but we still have a chance to make it. And red means unless we make a change, especially to scope, timeline, or resources, we won't make the plan.

I went with a green status on Project Blast, because on week one nothing had changed to make the plan not do-able. If we'd started out red or even yellow, it would've just inflamed the clients, and there was no action that could be taken that early in the project. The contract had just been signed and we just needed to start the work.

We also went with green so that if there were changes later that impacted the project, we could move the status to yellow or red and perhaps jointly agree to changes in the plan.

As I described earlier, there were several times in that project that we skirted certain disaster and pulled a rabbit out of a hat to stay on track. We never felt like exposing high risk to the clients would help us move forward faster, because there were still no actions they could take that would help us. And putting the project in red would put the clients on high alert and have them start micromanaging us and make it harder, not easier.

I also think the fact that we acted calm to the client, while working furiously in the background, gave them confidence and allowed us to work without them hovering over us.

Just to be clear, I'm not advocating always showing green status and hiding red. I am a big believer in using a red status if the project cannot achieve the current dates and especially if help is needed to get the project back on track. In that case, it would have just enraged the client and hindered progress.

## upward: your inner circle

You might want to distinguish what you tell your direct boss versus what you tell stakeholders from other groups.

On Project Blast, while I very intentionally didn't tell the consortium clients exactly how on the edge of failure we were, I was very open with my bosses and a board of directors that was assigned to meet with me weekly. I gave that inner circle of supporters all of the details of what was happening, as well as the challenges we were facing. I needed their input and advice on how to solve challenges. And I needed them to know how impossible a task they'd set before me. So, if we achieved it, they'd know how monumental of a task we'd achieved. And if we didn't achieve it, they'd know we'd tried our hardest and done everything we could.

Even if I reflected "green" to our client stakeholders, my inner circle knew we were bright yellow and on the verge of tipping over into red for most of the project.

## upward communications: if the company could be impacted

If there is a potential impact to the company or the project, then that's the cue to be open with the bosses, clients, or other stakeholders.

On a later project our task was to maintain old applications and keep them running for the company. It was a different mission than all of my previous projects, which had generally been to build new systems, but I had been brought in for the same reason as usual; things weren't going well. The team was severely undersized, and the structure of the team was intended to be cutting-edge and new, but that structure didn't work well with the ancient systems that were held together with baling wire and tape.

We struggled to get the right skills on the team because the skills required were old skills, not ones being taught in today's technical universities. We struggled to learn the systems because they were so old and poorly documented, and they had been running with "tribal knowledge" (a common term for knowledge gained over many years but not documented).

On that project, we didn't always tell the client if something went wrong if we were able to figure it out and fix it quickly, *and if* there wasn't an impact to the customers. They were already frustrated with us for not coming in and having the systems humming perfectly . . . so no need to expose to them every error we made.

If those errors could impact customers or the business, then we would be open with what happened and how, and we'd work with the client to fix everything.

## upward: no surprises

One of the best lessons I learned on Project Nebula from Bill was the need to socialize information prior to meetings. Socialize just means to review the material with people prior to the meeting so they aren't surprised by anything at the meeting. This is especially true the more senior the audience is, and the more contentious the material being discussed might be.

Why have the meeting then, if everyone has already seen the content ahead of time? Why not just meet with people individually and not do the meeting? It sounds like a lot of effort and useless work, right?

No, it's vital. I spent a lot of my time on Project Nebula meeting with people prior to the meetings, which allowed the meetings to be collaborative and decision-oriented, versus people being surprised by or frustrated by information. It allowed people to think through the decisions they'd be asked to make, rather than being forced to decide on the spot. Socialization was critical to the success of that program.

## downward communications: motivate and energize

I focus on telling my team everything that will motivate and energize them. When we are going through the hard work to fix and reset a team, I meet with the team frequently, at least monthly, if not more often, and give my team a rundown of all of the changes that are being made to the situation.

On Projects Falcon, Ascend and Blast, I held an All Hands meeting at least monthly to provide everyone on the team an update about the changes we were making to improve the Project, and about any positive feedback from the clients. It also gave the team a chance to ask any questions or make other suggestions. It was always helpful.

When I took over Mega Program Hydra with six different major towers, the situation was messy from the start. I did the same there, holding a monthly All Hands Meeting to provide my team with an understanding of the situation and the improvements we were making. The biggest problem we faced there was how the client "support functions" of legal, security, and network, were so aggressive they all but blocked our forward progress.

I found out my peers who were leading other towers weren't providing their teams the same communications. I only realized this when people from other towers would ask to join my All Hands just so they could get some information on how the leadership was trying to remove the blockades on our progress.

Anyone who wanted to join the meetings was welcome to attend, and they found it useful because nothing could be more frustrating than feeling like you're fighting an uphill battle without being sure that leadership is aware. Just knowing that leadership understood and were working with the clients to improve the situation was a huge motivator, even before any changes were implemented.

## downward communications: limit demotivation

I hold back from telling my team things that will demotivate and demoralize them, especially when it's not related to the actual work.

There is a divide between the day-to-day work of building or maintaining a system, versus the financial and administrative aspects that have very little to do with the actual work. Even in non-consulting worlds, there are politics related to funding of projects or fights for ownership and credit of work in organizations.

I will often shield my team from those politics or expose them only to a smaller group of leaders that I may need input from to solve the problems.

One clear example is that just as we were getting a major technical hurdle remediated on Project Ascend (the one for which we had to perform the root cause analysis), my bosses received an escalation letter from the president of the client company. The letter was extremely one-sided, and in an unprofessionally negative tone, it blamed my company for all of the technical hurdles. It was a clear case of both the software vendor and the client company trying to avoid any extra payments which we would be owed if the delays from the technical hurdles were the vendor's fault, and not ours. The letter was, in my opinion, not an act of good faith. It was a preemptive strike and was malicious, and it went straight to our senior leadership without us having a chance to discuss it first. I was gutted when I saw the letter, especially given that we were getting everything cleaned up and we were able to move forward.

I never, ever, shared the contents of that letter with anyone on my team. I let my junior leaders know that there was an escalation in progress but didn't go into details. And I never let the rest of my team know. The whole time it took to get that letter and the escalation resolved, I felt like I was being flayed alive, I was so upset. It seemed so unfair when my team had been working day and night to resolve the technical problem that we felt was primarily due to the software, or at least where there was joint responsibility.

I knew that the work would suffer and my team would be demoralized if they knew what was happening, and for the sake of the client, my company, and my team, I stayed silent and made sure the team kept working.

## downward communications: unprofessional, or non-specific negativity

I have worked with people in the past who haven't filtered feedback or politics from their team or their people, and instead just passed it through. I don't think that helps. If a client says they don't like a person on my team but don't provide professional feedback, I won't pass that on. If they have some specific feedback as to why they don't like the team member, I may give my team member specific actionable feedback about their behaviors, but I won't tell them that the client doesn't like them. Just because the client is being unprofessional doesn't mean I should do the same.

I had a new person on the Project Nebula team named Josh. He joined meetings but didn't take any notes, and it drove my client, Bill, crazy because Bill felt like Josh wasn't listening. Bill told me he didn't like Josh and to roll him off. I asked Josh about his lack of notetaking, and he said he was able to focus and listen better that way. He was getting the work done, so it was just a style difference. I told Josh that if Bill was in the room, to pretend to take a few notes, just to make him feel better. Josh took pretend notes from then on, scribbling in the margins, and he was on the team for several years and did a great job. I never told Josh that Bill didn't initially like him. That would have just made Josh uncomfortable and might have impacted his ability to do his work.

I said at the beginning of this chapter on communications that if action was needed, you should be open with your stakeholders and bring the action to them as early as possible.

"Asking for help" is a special form of "action" that I think needs to be addressed specifically. There are some nuances and considerations to be taken into account when asking for help.

## ASKING FOR HELP

In an earlier section I said, "If an action is needed, or a decision needs to be made, raise it up early and often." And I stand by what I said. But what if what you need is help. Is it okay to ask for help?

In my company, I heard multiple times that asking for help was a sign of strength, and the only leaders who really tanked their careers were those who didn't know when to ask for help and let a job go downhill. Those leaders who knew when to call in for help, if the job went well, were hailed for their maturity and calling for help was seen as a strength.

To be honest, I never really bought that philosophy, at least not to the extent that there would be no consequences at all for asking for help. Sure, asking for help and keeping a job out of the ditch is better than not asking for help and putting the job in the ditch. But . . . did I really believe the leader who asked for help was not going to be questioned as to why things went south in the first place?

So, when is it okay to ask for help, and from whom? Again, there is a difference if you're asking your team or your stakeholders for help.

### downward communications: help from the team

As a leader, it's your job to motivate and focus your team to solve challenges and accomplish the mission. So, what does asking for help from your team even mean? Aren't they always working with you and for you to achieve the mission? Doesn't everything they're doing constitute "help?"

Yes, but new challenges and problems can arise that you may need help with.

Why would you not ask your team for help?

Sometimes, I felt hesitant about asking my team for help, as I felt like my job was to protect them and they were often already doing too much.

Also, leaders are supposed to project an image of confidence that the mission can be achieved against all odds, so how does it look to the team when you go to them and ask for help and admit you don't know what to do?

If you ever watched the movie *U-571*, Jon Bon Jovi (yes, *that* Jon Bon Jovi) plays a Navy submarine captain who faces unsurmountable odds. At one point, he admits, "We'll never survive this." His NCO pulls him aside and tells him he needs to project confidence even if he doesn't have it. Spoiler alert: They figure it out.

Also, not asking your team risks losing their trust. I can't say we're in this together and then turn around and go to the big bosses for help without even letting them know there is a problem. And they could come up with a great solution I never thought of.

So, how do you ask your team for help without overburdening them, while also projecting confidence, so as not to demoralize them? It seems like a tightrope act.

First, be open about what the challenges are—at least with your cadre of next-level leaders. Those junior leaders will have a different perspective, as they're usually deeper into the details and may see other ways of solving the problem or other gaps that also need to be tackled. Make sure they understand the full context so they can make decisions based on where the real problems are.

Second, you can still project confidence—confidence that your team will bring the right ideas to figure things out, even if you don't know the solution yet.

On Project Blast, because of the tight timelines in the contract, we had to complete user experience testing (UAT) before the underlying architecture was going to be ready. We would be fined for every day we were late for UAT, so being late wasn't an option we could afford. I knew the team was working as fast as they could on the underlying platform, including on all of the security layers, so simply telling them to work faster wasn't going to solve the problem.

I sat down with a few of the leaders and asked, "Is there a way to still do UAT on time? What options do we have? Could we make a separate environment for just UAT? What if we didn't have to have security ready for the UAT environment?" We didn't specifically have to test for security during UAT, so if it wasn't there, it wouldn't really matter. What if we didn't have to have all of the architecture layers in place? I threw out a couple of ideas and questions to get the team thinking, fully believing we could come up with something which might work. But I didn't know the technology enough to know what was truly possible.

We ended up creating a parallel environment just for the webpages and interfaces, without all of the security layers. Having the separate environment allowed the security and infrastructure teams to continue their work unimpeded, while the functional team focused on the UAT environment.

Because we had a requirement for a 100 percent pass rate, we tested and re-tested the functionality ourselves on that separate environment, and we even brought in new joiners waiting for their first projects to test the site for us and make sure it looked correct and worked properly before the UAT.

That solution worked. We had the webpages tested so thoroughly that we passed UAT, and the architecture was allowed to be built properly without rushing it (more than we already had to) and opening ourselves for mistakes. Once the infrastructure was fully built, we were able to put the webpages on top of the full architecture and integrate them together.

Trusting the leads to solve yet another problem when they were already under fire helped the whole team. If I had just told them to hurry and hadn't confided in them what the real UAT goals were, I might have forced them to rush the security and could have exposed us to security breaches and much larger fines later.

Worse, if I hadn't gone to my team and decided to negotiate with the clients about the timeline instead, it could have exposed how tight we were on timelines. Working with my team and trusting them with the real need helped us thread yet another needle on that project.

## upward communications: factors beyond your control

After having exhausted all options with the team, and after having run options by them, there are times when it is appropriate to get help from the leadership, help from "up" the chain.

I'll be honest, I did that very sparingly. I can't ever remember asking for help from my leaders when I was in the military. You were given a mission to achieve, and you achieved it with the team of troops at your side. Maybe I could've asked for more equipment, and I once suggested a change to our schedule in Korea, architecting it myself, but I think in the military there was a culture of "get it done."

I asked one of my friends who was a colonel in the Air Force how asking for help up the chain was perceived in the military at the higher levels. He said, "I think it would depend on the reason the mission was not getting done. If it were due to *factors beyond your control*, then asking your leaders for help would be viewed positively."

Maybe because I had grown up with that military philosophy, or maybe because I was usually the one coming in to clean up a job that had gone badly, there weren't too many other places to turn for help. But I always believed that if the situation did not change due to factors "beyond my control," then I'd better control the situation and get it taken care of.

That said, there are a few things I learned about asking for help in the civilian world: when to do it, and perhaps more importantly, how to do it.

## upward communications: senior support

Regardless of how your company or project team is structured, having the right senior support is crucial. Your support may be your boss, or perhaps you could get support from a mentor or stakeholder from a different organization. The key is having someone available to you who can escalate to higher levels for you if needed, or who can negotiate some tricky situations that may occur. Regardless of how high you are in the organization, having the ear of someone more senior and more experienced is critical for your success. If you don't have that person in your corner, you need to find them.

In Project Ascend, Brad was our program sponsor. Brad was a seasoned executive who was a step above me in the organization, and who had years more experience. Brad had a great relationship with one of the C-level leaders at the client company and was able to meet with him to discuss some of the challenges we were having and get them resolved behind the scenes.

Brad was also great at listening, understanding, and providing sage advice on how to navigate a situation. Without the support of Brad and his relationships at the client, we might not have been successful there.

## upward communications: get others in the boat with you

Similar to having senior support, it's always good to have leadership "in the boat with you," so they're there if things go wrong.

Project Blast was so risky from the outset that I had a set of senior leaders volunteer to be on what was essentially a board of directors to meet with me weekly. They questioned me about what we were doing and how it was going, and they gave me advice.

At the beginning it was rough because there were multiple voices all questioning me or telling me to do various things, when I felt like I knew what needed to be done. But I kept meeting with them, and we eventually got into a good rhythm. There were things that they advised that were really critical, and they could also help to get me resources if there was a gap.

If the project had gone poorly, they couldn't claim that I hadn't done everything in my power, because they were essentially at my side through the whole process. And, since the project did go well, they knew what we had gone through and all of the challenges we'd fought and won, which helped me because they were able to vouch for me during performance reviews. Having leadership at your side is never a bad thing, and having their fingerprints on the project can only help, especially when things get rocky.

## upward communications: specific skills

Fairly soon after I took over Project Ascend, the client wanted to do a new contract with fixed timelines and delivery dates to hold my company accountable. The client had written a draft contract that was super one-sided, assuming everything was our fault, and the clients were going to make sure that if we put a single toe out of line in the future we'd pay for it. But the reality was that we needed to make sure that the contract held the client accountable for limits on requirements, since one of the main problems with the program was they didn't know what they really needed. Anyone who says: "We don't know what our objectives are, but we're aligned on them," needs to be held accountable too.

Negotiating the contract wasn't going to be something that I could handle alone.

We called up the ladder to get support from our negotiation center, a set of specialists in negotiating hard contracts. We got a negotiator assigned, and he was able to reset expectations and reset the tone. It was still a months long negotiation, during which I had to work through the details of the contract that I would have to deliver. At least I had an expert to help us get through the tricky parts, including penalties and liabilities.

## upward communications: have a point of view

Going to your boss with a clear opinion of what you need and why is a very different scenario from going to your boss and saying, "I need help, but I don't know what I need." Or even worse, "My project is all messed up, but I don't know why."

Again, on Project Ascend, we had to redo the architecture of the application, and we had a lot of tech debt that we needed to remediate. The architect on the project was very good at compiling a list of all of the things we needed to do, but he was super analytical and detailed, like an absent-minded professor, and he couldn't direct the team to get those things done.

The lead that I had on the team was very good at managing the team administratively, but he wasn't technical, so he didn't know how to prioritize the list or who could work on what.

I had a major gap in someone who could both direct the team and who had the right level of technical knowledge. That role was, of course, not planned into our project, and that kind of skilled person was hard to find, as the good resources are always in high demand.

I escalated that need to SubCo leadership and had to be able to say both why I needed that person, as well as why the architect and the current lead couldn't do the role. I had to keep pushing up the chain to get to the right level of leadership to get someone assigned. The person who ended up joining our project did it very much against his will, as it required him to fly from Seattle to Connecticut to work with us. We worked out a deal with him where he could come every other week and kept his time on site to two or three days a week.

He was perfect for the role, and I made a point of building a relationship with him. Because of his skill, we were able to burn down the list of technical tasks and got the application stable and singing.

By the end of the project, he said he'd learned a lot on the role and he was a big part of our "family party". If I hadn't pushed for his role to be filled and been very specific about what we needed, I'm not sure the project would have been successful. (I realize I've said that several times. But a lot of things had to come together to make that project successful in the end!)

The bottom line is, the larger the team you are leading, and the more complex the activity your team is responsible for, the higher the likelihood that you and your team will need help. As a leader, your job is to make sure the objectives are met and to support the team to do them. "Troops eat first" may mean that you need to get them help, and to do so you'll need to have senior relationships in the organization you're working in. You'll need to know when and how to ask for help, and what to ask for. Doing so may be crucial to your team's success.

# 5.

# MANAGING YOUR CAREER

Why is "managing your career" a relevant discussion for a leader? Many people think that a leader should just focus on their team and their objectives. If they do a good job leading their team, that should be enough.

I believe that two questions should be considered when it comes to managing a career. The first is "Why?" A leader should first ask themselves why they want to move up. What's the value of getting to the higher levels? If one likes leading teams, they should consider whether they even want to go higher in the ranks.

The second question is if a leader wants to get promoted and move up, why can't they just do a good job? The upper leadership should notice that the leader is good and move them up, right? Let's unpack these questions in-depth below.

## WHY MOVE UP?

As a leader, why push for promotion?

Of course, promotions come with increased pay and benefits, recognition for hard work, and not getting passed up by others (competition can be a great motivator!). But all of those things are drivers for promotions across the board, and are not specific to leaders.

And, while career growth used to be an assumed path, numerous articles question whether it still is, especially for

Gen Z, which is more likely to say 'no' to taking leadership positions, as they obviously come with higher responsibility and likely longer hours.[3]

As a leader, there are some specific benefits of moving into the higher levels. The first is the ability to lead a bigger team. The bigger the team, the more people you can support and influence. I had teams that spanned from 3 to 4 people in my first years as a consultant, and those numbers reached up to 150 to 200 on some of my later projects. I liked the larger projects, which required many different skills and personalities to accomplish our objectives. We would have a wide range of levels, from new joiners to seasoned experts, and people often came from different backgrounds. I appreciated being able to support them both in terms of the project and in terms of their career goals.

The second benefit of career advancement is greater challenges. With the larger projects, I felt like I was constantly learning and being challenged to keep everyone working together and keep the project moving forward. I was given Project Falcon, my first recovery project, just after I got promoted to the executive level. I never would have been able to do that role without getting promoted, and it set me on the "fixer" trajectory that was to define the rest of my career.

Third, with more seniority comes a stronger voice in the company and a greater ability to impact outcomes. When I took over Project Ascend, I had just gotten promoted to the next executive level, and I felt truly empowered to make decisions, including telling the account lead to step away and let me lead.

Lastly, I think the more senior you are, the greater the ability you have to mentor or sponsor people's career growth. Without being at the right level of the organization, you won't be able to sponsor the people who you feel most deserving of promotion.

For me, I love being a leader and wanted to continue to grow and keep taking on larger teams.

## know the demands of the next level

The best way to be promoted is to be doing the activities required for the next level. If you're already demonstrating the skills and the capabilities of the next level, it will be much easier to promote you. And it's also critical to understand what the next level will require of you, so that you can determine if that is something you want.

A recent *Fortune* article noted that, "29% of workers who were promoted left within a month—compared with just 18% for those who weren't."[4] The implications are obvious, that the people who are getting promoted don't necessarily know what they're getting into and aren't prepared for it, or they just don't enjoy it.

I knew one person in IT—Jerry—who refused to become a manger. That is a career limiting move in IT, where a lot of the individual contributor tech work can be done overseas in India or elsewhere for a fraction of the cost. But Jerry stuck to his guns and stayed an individual contributor. He took roles with the federal government as a contractor (as US rules prohibit the use of offshore workers). Certainly, he made less money than if he had become a manager, but he was probably happier than if he'd taken the promotion to manager and then hated it. He would have been one of those 29 percent who quit immediately after getting promoted.

As an IT executive myself, Jerry's decision to stay an individual contributor always seemed bizarre to me. But now I admire him for knowing himself enough to make that call. He would have been just as unhappy as a leader as I would have been as an individual contributor. I was raised through the military to be a leader and in my earlier career, when I didn't have troops to lead, I pushed through it but didn't love it. I am only grateful that they promoted me up to the levels where I could lead teams and come into my own.

As I grew more senior in my career, while I was able to lead larger and larger teams in my company, I also acquired additional expectations related to sales. Some people I know chose to stay at the lower levels where they could lead smaller teams, but not have as much focus on sales.

There is no right or wrong answer when it comes to being promoted or not. My advice is to make sure you understand what the requirements of the next level are, and start trying to fulfill those requirements if you want to be promoted, or reconsider your path if you don't.

## doing your job is not managing your career

In our company, and in the companies of all of the clients I worked with, you needed to take the reins of your career in hand and drive and manage it if you wanted to get to the higher levels. People who assume they'll get promoted if they do a good job often get overlooked, especially to get into the executive levels.

At the Air Force Academy, I had to memorize a quote by General George S. Patton that said, "If I do my full duty, the rest will take care of itself." More than memorize it, I felt like it was woven into the very fiber of my being. I was not unique in that. Duty in the military is an almost holy concept. Doing our duty is not just something we do, it's who we are. Recently, a former military colleague from my consulting company posted that quote on LinkedIn.

When I first joined the company, I followed the same standard because I so firmly believed that "the rest" would happen if I did my job, my duty, to the fullest.

Except it's not true. In the civilian world (and frankly in the military world as well) the career trajectory doesn't always "take care of itself."

On Project Ascend, a senior manager named Brian and I arrived to the project on the same day. Brian was two steps below me on the corporate ladder, and he and a handful of other leaders at his level would be my right-hand people through the recovery.

Brian was fantastic, one of the most solid leaders I'd worked with in a long time, if not ever. He was calm under pressure, had no fear of having hard conversations with the clients, and was able to raise issues with such calm rationality that the clients rarely got upset and worked with him to resolve the problems. He was supportive of his team and spent time getting to know each individual. He was in charge of one of the two major workstreams we had running, and his focus on the second workstream allowed me to spend time with the first, which was extremely messy.

Brian was also former military. Though his experience in the Air Force was very different than my own, we approached leadership very similarly. By seniority, he should have been ready for promotion to the executive level.

In our firm, as in many companies, promotion to the executive levels is not just a stairstep but an almost seismic shift, and it requires more than just doing an excellent job. It requires having the right network and sponsors, and it takes a thorough marketing of one's readiness for that level. Working hard may result in promotion in the lower ranks, but that stops at the executive levels. Marshall Goldsmith's *What Got You Here Won't Get You There* is an excellent book which delves into this concept much deeper.

A former classmate of mine who'd made it to the rank of colonel in the Air Force and who found the same to be true in the military, used this analogy: Getting to colonel or general (which are equivalent to executive levels in the civilian world) requires a sponsor taking an interest in you, and putting you on the on-ramp to those leadership levels.

If you don't have that support, you could continue to drive on the side roads for your whole career and never get past lieutenant colonel.

Brian was at that exact same point in his career, wanting to make the jump from senior manager to the executive level of managing director, but he didn't know what he needed to do to get there. He was just "doing his full duty," keeping his head down, and was so busy doing his "job" that he wasn't managing his career.

I found in working with a veteran group at my company that most veterans had a similar attitude. They had swallowed the "duty" concept and never considered having to market themselves to get to the next level. There is also a concept in the military that the person who stands the tallest gets cut down, meaning that standing out and being better than everyone else in a military unit is frowned upon. A military unit is supposed to act as one, in harmony, as someone who is trying to get ahead and not staying "in step" with everyone else can be a liability in battle.

I got that lesson very early on. Prior to joining the Air Force Academy, I had been given a copy of the Contrails book of military knowledge that freshmen are supposed to memorize during basic training. I had memorized many of the paragraphs-long quotes, prior to entering basic training, which gave me a huge leg up. During basic training, when we were told "Schofield's quote. Go!" I knew I was about to shine. Schofield's quote is the longest, and hardest to memorize, and it put fear into the hearts of every basic cadet.

When quotes are said in basic training, all twenty to twenty-five basic cadets of the flight have to say them in unison, with a cadence, as a way of building unity and perhaps beating down one's sense of individuality. I started to rattle off the quote, a bit louder and faster than my classmates. When they stumbled I kept on going, and instead of being lauded for my amazing knowledge of the quote, I was yelled at for standing out, for making my classmates look bad. I got hazed for trying to show off. It was the last time I made that mistake.

So, it's no wonder that shifting from a military career to a civilian career, it's tough to market oneself, to push for one's own promotion, to stand up and announce that you deserve the promotion over your fellow colleagues.

I also found that women were more likely than men to be so focused on their "jobs" that they weren't focusing on their careers. They also tended to believe that if they did a good job they'd be rewarded for it and keep moving up the ladder. That is also part of women's cultural upbringing in the US, not to stand out, not to be seen as too pushy or demanding, and not bragging about oneself.

But the reality is that for everyone, veteran, men, and women, if you don't push for your promotion, those who do will pass you by. If you don't take your career by the horns and drive yourself forward, you'll stay where you are on the sideroads.

I sat Brian down and explained the system, and we charted out a course for what he would need to do to get the right support and get on the superhighway. I would be a mentor for him for several years until he got there. I connected dots for him, made intros for him, encouraged him, and counseled him, but ultimately, he needed to spend the time managing his career in order to get there, while continuing do his job.

If you are at all like I was in my junior years, or if you're like so many of the people on my teams who needed to be coached into managing their careers, you may finally realize that you need to manage your career. But you may still not know HOW to do it. What do you have to do?

## sponsorship versus mentorship

I mentioned briefly that you need to find a sponsor who will support you and get you onto the on-ramp to the executive levels. Couldn't I have done that for Brian in my last example? Is a sponsor the same as a mentor? No, a sponsor is more than just a mentor.

A mentor is someone who wants to help and will provide you guidance and advice but doesn't have the seniority or the right position in the company to make inroads for you. A sponsor is senior enough to open doors for you, introduce you to the right people, and advocate on your behalf in promotion discussions. Ideally, you'll have both mentors and sponsors.

When I was pushing for promotion to the executive levels, I didn't know anything about what it really took to get there. Fortunately, I had someone who I had worked with for the better part of my career who was acting as a true sponsor.

Marty knew what I needed to do to get the visibility with the decision-makers for promotion so they could know me and know my capabilities. Marty told me to meet with my practice lead in order to provide him a bi-weekly summary of our account's technology sales opportunities and delivery status. I 100 percent believed that the practice lead was getting his information from other sources and this was a thinly-veiled opportunity for me to get some visibility with him. I was also wise enough to take the opportunity seriously, and I demonstrated a good understanding of all of our delivery challenges and sales progress in each session.

I got promoted that year, and despite all of the hard work I was doing on delivery, I know that I would not have gotten promoted without connecting with the practice lead, in addition to all of my sponsor's support. A mentor, by contrast, would have told me to get time with the practice lead, but they would not have been in a position to create that bi-weekly meeting for me. I had another sponsor later in my career who got me to the next step on the executive ladder. I'll cover his actions in the "Level the Career Playing Field" section.

## don't assume everyone knows what you're doing

So many people believe that doing great work will lead to career growth and promotion. That may be true in a small organization or small business where your boss works with you all day long. In large corporations, and especially in the modern world of remote working, hybrid working (partially remote, partially in the office), or when your boss may work out of a different office, the reality is your boss may not know all of the things you're doing, all of the potential crises you averted, or the great ideas that you brought to the table. The only way to make sure your boss knows all of the things you did is to tell him or her. Honestly, even if your boss saw everything, more than likely your boss has multiple people reporting to them and there's no way they can remember everything about every person on their team.

How exactly you'll provide that information to your boss may vary based on your corporate culture. For example, you could send an email summarizing a key outcome like resolving a conflict, after it is resolved. You could also send a summary of your contributions for the quarter or year, providing both the numerical stats like sales, revenue, widgets completed, etc., but also the qualitative contributions like new ideas, team members coached, or team accomplishments.

For those of you that are shaking your head and thinking you can't ring your own bell or brag like that, you need to know that others in your organization will have no issue telling everyone everything they've done, including taking credit for 100 percent of an outcome, no matter how little they contributed to it. If you aren't telling your stakeholders all of the contributions you're making, they may not know and the promotion you deserve based on your contributions may go to someone who is more vocal.

There was a leader named Ian on my Project Falcon team who was originally from the United Kingdom but was working in the United States. He was pushing to get to the next level, and he was competing for promotion slots against other leaders from North America. He was doing a great job, managing a complex area, and getting results in terms of sales and revenue. He sent in an end of year report summarizing all of his accomplishments but didn't get the promotion he thought he deserved. I had just taken over the team at that point and resolved to help him get the visibility he needed to get promoted.

We talked about his communication style and when he would talk to his boss. As we talked things through over several sessions, I realized he was still operating according to UK standards, but he was being measured against US employees who were operating differently. In the UK, the standard was to handle things in your area and never go to the boss unless there was something he absolutely needed. Handling things very independently was prized, and the outcomes would show the quality of his work. But in the US, because his area was perceived as so "quiet" it was thought to be "less complex," so even though he got the same sales and revenue numbers as others it was deemed "easier" for him, and the promotion spots went to others.

The other thing, culturally, was that "bragging" was perceived as even less acceptable in the UK, and Ian was averse to anything that smacked of bragging or patting himself on the back. The end of year summary, something most considered required and the absolute minimum of documentation, was the only *self-promotion* acceptable to him by UK standards.

We decided to try a new method. He would send an email to his boss whenever a potential crisis happened. Something to the effect of, "Hey boss, I wanted to let you know that this crisis is happening. I believe I can handle it by doing X and Y, and I'll let you know if I need any help." And then, when the crisis was handled, he could send a follow-up note saying, "Hey boss, regarding that potential crisis, it has been solved by X, Y, and Z actions, and the client is now happy. Let me know if you have any questions."

Despite shaking his head and thinking it was the loopiest plan ever, Ian agreed to try it. Throughout the year, Ian wrote several such sets of emails and was credited for numerous crises averted. His boss realized how challenging his area was to manage, and that despite that complexity, Ian continued to turn in solid sales and revenue numbers. Ian was promoted in the next yearly cycle.

Ian had already been doing great work, but it wasn't until he started keeping his boss in the loop and making sure the boss really understood his contributions that he got the promotion he deserved.

So, ask yourself, "Does your boss really understand what you are doing?"

## know who is making the decision

The reality is, there may be many people who need to understand your contributions, not just your boss. You need to find out who makes promotion decisions, and that answer will vary based on your organization.

If you don't know who is making the decision, how can you be sure they'll give you a good rating or promote you? It's easy to believe that your boss or supervisor has the power to decide, and that if they love your work they'll promote you. In a small organization that may be true.

In many large corporations, however, there are committees and practice-owners and matrixed leadership structures that will make the decision. It is even more important as you move up in the ranks, and especially moving into the executive or C-levels, as those levels typically need broad organizational support, and assuming your boss has the kind of power necessary to promote you to those levels by his or her word alone, is likely to leave you stranded at the lower levels.

Which means that, you need to understand exactly who is on the committees or panels who will be deciding on your career, and the more you can get to know them, and get them to know you and to understand the work you're doing and the importance to the company, the better.

If you already know them, it may be as simple as copying them on some of the emails you're sending to your boss about your work. If you don't know them already, you may need to work harder to get them to know you.

And, of course, that may be easier said than done, as the people who are on the committees at those levels don't have time to meet with every single person who is trying to get promoted. If that's your case, you may need help getting the right introductions or opportunities to interact with them. That's where you need a sponsor who can help you through the correct steps to get the right visibility.

I had a person on my team who was trying to figure out his next role, as his role on the project ended. He had a couple of different technical roles he could do, but I knew they were bad for his career. He thought the roles sounded interesting, so he couldn't understand why I was pushing him to consider other roles.

I explained the various practices, showed him where he currently belonged, and explained by whom and how the career and rating decisions were made. He was in an industry practice but was considering deeply technical roles that should come from our architecture practice. He didn't understand that he would still be judged against the people in industry practice, and that the deep tech skills he would develop weren't relevant for the industry practice. He either needed to switch to the architecture practice or pick roles that would be more valued by his industry practice.

This is a conversation I've had with people I've mentored dozens of times. The striking part about it this time was that he was at a level in his career where he should have known his practice and how he was being judged. He had no idea, and was just happy to keep doing "a good job." That may have worked when he was more junior, but doing a good job at the wrong role could be career-impacting at the senior level he was at.

In a second example, one of the clients that I worked with was pushing for the executive levels and kept being told by her boss that he would support her, but he wasn't being open with her and didn't help her understand the broad committee of people who would need to be aligned in the decision to promote her. Only after pushing the point with him did she get a better idea of the approving committee, as well as an introduction to one of the key stakeholders on the committee.

## know what you're being measured on, focus on it, and limit anything else

Ask whoever is going to provide your ratings what they will be measuring you on. Despite how obvious that sounds, you'd be surprised by how many people don't do it. Possibly because they feel stupid asking because they feel like they should know. Or because they feel they shouldn't have to ask. The boss will know if I'm doing a good job, right?

Don't you think you'll feel more stupid at the end of the year when you get a less-than-stellar rating, if it turns out you weren't focused on the things your boss thought you should be?

But, shouldn't the boss tell you that you're not doing the right things? Shouldn't he or she give you feedback? See the upcoming "Giving Feedback" section for more details, but no, don't assume that. Some people don't like giving feedback, especially when someone isn't living up to their expectations, because it can be painful. So, don't assume they'll tell you you're not doing a good job, and don't assume you are doing the right things. Ask what you'll be measured on, and then focus on those things.

For example, if at the end of the year you are going to be measured on sales, or revenue or headcount hired or number of training modules created or delivered, then your primary focus should be on doing those things.

If you boss asks you to do other duties, think carefully before accepting those extra duties. These can be anything such as doing interviews, training new hires, organizing happy hours or monthly birthday cakes, or organizing "lunch and learn" sessions.

Consider a few points: Does everyone else at your level or in your role have a few extra duties? Or are you the only one being "gifted" with them?

If everyone has some extra duties, then ask if you can choose a meaty extra duty, for example, interviewing new candidates or training new hires may show more of your leadership skills, knowledge of the company, and potential for advancement versus other roles like organizing happy hours. Then, make sure the performance of those extra duties doesn't interfere with your ability to focus on and complete the tasks you'll be measured on.

For women in particular, these extra duties can be onerous. There is an unconscious bias that often causes people (both men and women) to ask women to do the extra chores, from taking notes, organizing meetings, and setting up social events, while the men are given the more important tasks that will lead them to get better ratings.

I had a friend call me for some advice regarding her workplace, which was at a pharmaceutical company. She was frustrated with her role and that a man was hired into a position more senior than hers, even though he had less experience, and she had ticked every experience box possible. She asked my advice on how to show her bosses that she should be promoted and be operating at a more senior level.

She told me that one of the things she was doing to show leadership was organizing happy hours and monthly birthday celebrations to bring the team together and foster a better work environment. I was glad I was talking to her via cell phone and not on video, because I think I actually grimaced.

I told her, "Be very careful of those kinds of activities. Everyone will be very happy to come eat the cake or go out for drinks, but no one is going to think you're a leader because of it. It will be seen as administrative, and it may even diminish you in their eyes. Would one of those guys who is so focused on promotion spend any amount of work time organizing events? No, they'll let the women do that and focus their time on their research."

I told her that what she needed to do was tell her boss that she's ready to take the next role, and that she has the qualifications to do it. And to ask him directly if there was anything else she needed to do to demonstrate readiness.

She stopped doing the happy hours and birthday cakes and instead had direct conversations with her boss about her promotability. She was promoted about six months later and was much happier to be working at a level in line with her level of experience.

## opportunity versus loyalty

Specifically in consulting, there is a cardinal rule that you can never roll yourself off a project. You are on the project and doing the project until you are rolled off, whether because the role is completed or the project finishes or for performance reasons. The only exception to this is you can get pulled from the project by a senior leader, and that senior leader would need to get agreement with your current leadership. Getting pulled is okay. Stepping out is never okay.

With that rule as context, you may recall I was leading a very large team on a Mega Program called Hydra. We had essentially taken over the IT department of a company and were doing several large system implementations and were driving all of their projects. We had divided up the work into six major pillars, and I was leading one of the six. At that time, it was the largest project in the firm.

I had over 200 people on my team, and my team was running 30 projects concurrently. I had taken the role because I was trying to move to the next level of leadership, and I was convinced that it would give me the right level of responsibility.

There were a lot of things going wrong on Hydra. Four of the six other pillars were in pretty bad shape and additional leaders had been brought in to help. There were budget overruns, and we were behind on our timelines. The client was frustrated with how things were going and wasn't taking any accountability for some of the obstacles their own organization was putting in our path.

In my area, things were going well, and we were generally meeting both budget and timelines.

At one point, I called Joe, a senior expert in customer relationship management (CRM), to come talk to my lead client. I had interacted with him briefly in the past and knew he was extremely credible and thought my client would like him. My client at the time was very pragmatic and would sniff out and turn her nose up at anything "salesy" in an instant.

Joe and I met with her, and as he was telling her all about the latest CRM trends, she looked at me. I knew that look. It was, "What do you think? Is this right?" I was not the CRM expert, but I trusted Joe. I wouldn't have brought him to meet her if he wasn't good. I nodded at her.

Joe was extremely perceptive and noticed our interaction. He told me later he knew I was "the real deal" when he saw my client look to me for confirmation before believing a word he said.

Joe met with my client a few times over the next few weeks, and on one of his visits he told me I'd be great at leading a new project he was on the cusp of selling at another client. The implication was that he would pull me if I had agreed.

I turned down his opportunity because I thought I was needed where I was. I felt like I would be letting my team down.

Later, I regretted turning down Joe's offer. I saw the person who took the role get promoted to the next level. On my project, while my pillar was going well, the rest of the program was a mess. My boss retired and a new leader took over who was far from a people person and who was so focused on the failing pillars that he took no notice of me.

He told me from the beginning, "Your area seems well managed, so I won't be spending much time with you." While that should have made me happy it meant he had no idea what I was really doing, and he was so mired in fixing the rest of the job that I had no support for promotion.

That project taught me several lessons. First, even if it is supposedly a good role, you still need the right visibility, marketing, and sponsorship to get to the next level. I did not have the right visibility. (My boss was too focused on the failing areas.) I wasn't doing a good job marketing myself, and I had no sponsor.

The second thing I learned is that loyalty is good, but you have to know when to cut the cords and move on. I should have seen that the opportunity that Joe was offering me also came with his sponsorship. I know this because after that "miss" I didn't say no when he offered me his sponsorship and another project a few years later. Only because I accepted his sponsorship, did I make it to the next level.

## do your job; push the boundaries

One of the best pieces of advice I was given in my early years was "Don't just do what you're asked. If you do what we ask and that's it, you'll get an 'average' rating. You have to do more."

As I grew in my career, I leveraged that advice and told all of the people that I mentored, "Do your job, then push the boundaries."

Do your job. There is a need and there is value in you doing it, otherwise they wouldn't be paying you to do it. So you have to make sure that the things you've been asked to do get done. The reason I start with this is that sometimes people will be so focused on promotion or on doing additional things that they don't get the basics done.

There was one salesman I worked with who seemed to be focused on everything but the fundamentals of his job which was sales. He kept worrying about how to build a better relationship with his boss (Sell more!), and he kept trying to distinguish himself from the other salesmen by finding new, interesting clients and companies. (Interesting is only good if they buy, and spend lots of dollars. Boring current clients who spend lots of dollars will win over interesting new clients who don't buy as much every time. More dollars is more better in sales.) He was also very focused on extra duties like supporting various people activities which are all good, but his focus was all wrong.

Do your job. Hit your numbers. Do the things you've been assigned.

Then push the boundaries and do your job bigger and better than asked. That can be selling thirty widgets when they've asked you to sell twenty, or it can be designing a system that not only meets the business case of getting rid of the old server-based systems, but also reduces the training time for the users, reduces the number of order fallouts, and increases user engagement. Whatever it is, do what they've asked, and then do more; do better than what they've asked.

## are you being valued?

If you've decided you want to be promoted, and if you're doing everything you can to manage your career, and if you're still not getting promoted, maybe you're not in the right place. Really consider what you want and ask if your company values what you do.

One of my clients was pushing for the VP ranks, but she kept getting passed by. The feedback from her boss in terms of what else she needed to do to show readiness for VP wasn't specific or clear. It seemed to me that either he didn't support her, or at least he had others he wanted to promote first.

If you're in the situation where you see people passing you by for promotions, ask yourself if you're taking all of the steps to manage your career. Do you know what you are measured on; are you marketing yourself; do you have a sponsor?

If you have done all of the things that you think should be done and believe you have demonstrated everything needed for promotion, but you still keep getting passed by, consider moving to a different department so that you can get a different boss and, hopefully, a sponsor.

Or, you may also consider moving to a different company.

The bottom line is that if you feel you are demonstrating everything you believe is needed to be promoted, and you've had the specific conversations about what else is needed and you're not getting traction, perhaps you're not in the right spot where your talents can shine and be recognized.

Let me share another example. I was always a delivery person. I loved building large teams and tackling complex projects. I loved walking into a chaotic situation, figuring out how to bring order to the chaos. But my company always valued sales more than delivery. I managed to make it to our executive levels through delivery, but I always felt like a fish swimming upstream, and my path would have been much swifter if I had just turned around and focused on sales instead. But I didn't like sales, and I wasn't good at sales. I did enough sales to get me through to each next level, but it was not my passion.

For a time, I tried to help change the culture to value delivery more. And sometimes the company would say they valued delivery. But they always valued sales more. And while there were many factors at play when I decided to step out and retire, one of them was that who I was at my core, a delivery person, wasn't valued as highly as I felt like it should be.

Everyone has to manage their careers. If you don't, you may be passed for promotion by others who aren't better at "the job" but are better at "the career."

However, as we saw earlier, the playing field is not level for everyone. There are some specific considerations to take into account for managing the career for women and other diversity groups.

## LEVEL THE CAREER PLAYING FIELD

Earlier in the book, I covered "Level the Playing Field," which specifically focused on how a leader should ensure all players on the team are treated equally and to harness each of their unique capabilities. The focus of that section was more about making the playing field level for doing the "job."

In this section, I'll focus on leveling the playing field for career management. There are a few factors that can impact women's careers if they aren't on guard and actively managing their career. And, frankly, if they don't have the right support and sponsorship to overcome the biases, even actively managing their career may not be enough.

### women's work may be seen as more administrative

I provided a few examples earlier in the book illustrating that women tend to be given more administrative work or extra duties, whether taking notes or setting up happy hours. They also may be given more administrative roles versus technical ones.

Getting the right role is a critical first step to career progression. However, even when a woman has a role that is meaty and/or technical, she still might be *assumed* (incorrectly) to be doing an administrative role, because of the same unconscious biases that guide people to give women administrative work.

On the Mega Program Hydra where I was given one of the six pillars to lead, all of my peers on the other five units were male. It was an extremely challenging environment and problems started happening almost immediately. On several of the other units a second leader was added, but I continued to lead my pillar on my own. Several of the other pillars had such problems that we ended up having to negotiate with the clients in terms of payments and losses.

My area continued to deliver projects on time, and essentially to the expected margins, and I had good relationships with my clients. My pillar even sold strategic new work. (Something which was a rarity because of the way the overall Mega Program was structured.) I even held an innovation session for my clients, where the rest of my colleagues' projects were in flames, and they were just trying to keep their heads above water.

At the end of that performance year, two of my male colleagues were promoted to the level I was striving for, even though their portions of the work were either canceled or went so badly the individuals were rolled off from the program.

I was not promoted and was only given an average rating, the worst rating of my career.

Compared to my peers on that crazy program, I was knocking it out of the park. I asked my boss what happened, and he said the higher-level leadership believed that I was a program manager, essentially a non-technical lead, compared to all of the other (male) leaders who were technical delivery leaders. I was doing exactly the same work as my peers, only better. But I was the only woman. I was assumed to be doing non-technical work, which was purely due to the unconscious bias that women do administrative work.

I felt like my legs had been kicked out from under me. Especially because, as I said in the previous chapter, I had chosen to stay on the Hydra Mega Program versus taking the role that Joe would have pulled me onto. That's because I thought this was a good role for me, and I thought they needed me.

I think the real killer for my promotion that year was the fact that I didn't have a sponsor at that point. The boss who I thought was supporting me didn't have enough heft to correct the senior leadership's view of me. And I had turned down Joe's sponsorship (unwittingly) by turning down the role he offered me. I'll cover more on sponsorship for women later in this section.

The bottom line is, even if a woman has a meaty role, she may need to prove that the work she's doing is as meaty and as challenging as her peers' roles. She may need to prove her worth over and over, even if her colleagues pass by on an assumption of competence. If you are her supervisor, you'll need to make sure the upper levels truly understand what she was doing.

It's exactly like what I saw in the military. I was questioned as to whether I could carry my weapon, but it was assumed that all of my (male) colleagues would do just fine.

## untapped potential

Sheryl Sandberg, in *Lean In: Women, Work, and the Will to Lead,* said something that absolutely resonated with me: "Men are promoted based on potential, while women are promoted based on past accomplishments." After that year when I was passed by for promotion on the Mega Program Hydra, it would take me years to get the promotion I wanted. I had to prove over and over again that I was doing the same technical role as my male colleagues and that I was ready for the next level of leadership.

The main reason for this is that people tend to want to support people who are like them. They promote people based on potential, because they remind them of themselves at that level. And, because a lot of leaders in the corporate world are still men, and these leaders tend to see potential in men like them.

In the military, we used to say leaders who got promoted based on potential "look good in the uniform," meaning, those people are promoted who seem to embody the presence of a military leader, even if they haven't actually demonstrated it. Even if they weren't great leaders. (Those leaders were always men.)

I've seen the same thing with some executives that have figured out how to use the right expressions and have the right presence. They make the right connections, find the right sponsors, and are in the right place at the right time, and even though they didn't carry a major sale on their back or lead a project, people believed in them enough that they got promoted.

Some might say, "So what?" Yes, they have figured out how to play the game and they were promoted because of it, and that's exactly the point. They're playing the game by a different set of rules than women have.

The best (Worst!) example I've seen of this was at a client company. There was a female director trying to get to the VP level. She finally quit the company when the boss made it clear to her that she would never get VP. The job for her replacement, covering all of the areas she had been responsible for, was posted at the VP level. A male who had no experience with any of the areas she had managed was promoted into the role as a VP.

The newly promoted VP had no experience in those areas and spent the first year struggling in his role. And the woman who left had been managing all of those areas for years.

So, what can be done about this imbalance in promotion?

## get a sponsor

I covered the criticality of getting a sponsor in the "Managing Your Career" section. Because sponsorship can be especially challenging for women, I want to highlight a few additional points here. Another *Harvard Business Review* study found that "Women are over-mentored and under-sponsored."[5]

I had a great sponsor, Marty, who helped me get from the senior manager level to the executive level. But then I made the decision to join the Mega Program Hydra and I moved out of Marty's sphere of influence. I spent many years after that struggling to get the right roles and the recognition for what I was doing, and I got passed by for the next level multiple times. I watched a peer who had been junior to me pass me by because he was being sponsored and supported by the leader of his technology group.

I was given a lot of advice, like what role to take, that I should get certified in a specific technology, and that I should make sure I told my reporting structure what I was doing. But nothing seemed to get me to the next level. It was never enough, or the right people never took notice. I even had a boss write a nice email upon his retirement, telling the leadership to "take care of" me, which, along with five dollars, would buy me a cup of coffee.

Finally, I ran into Joe at a networking event. (We'll cover the value of networking in the next section.)

I had run into Joe a few times throughout my career, but I hadn't seen him for at least a year since I'd turned down the program he offered to me while I was on Hydra. I had been working hard, and doing a good job, but I was essentially invisible to anyone who mattered. I didn't know how to market myself; I didn't know what to do to be heard. And I was still trying to overcome the bias that I was more of a program manager versus a technical delivery leader.

Based on some of the things he'd seen in me over the years, Joe decided to sponsor me. He pulled me out of the roles I was doing and asked me to take on Project Blast, the five-month website build. Project Blast was hard enough and impactful enough to my company that if I got it right, I would finally be seen as a technical delivery leader, and I might finally get to the next level. When I delivered the project two days early, I got the promotion that I had been struggling to get.

Without Joe's sponsorship, both in terms of the right role, and in terms of visibility with the right leadership levels, I probably wouldn't have gotten there or it would have taken even longer.

## get men involved

Since men sit in many of the top leadership roles of companies, they need to be brought into the discussion. Most men I have met want to help; they want women to succeed. They sometimes just don't know what to do about it. Men need to be included and engaged and educated on the challenges that women face so they can be part of the solution.

In a women's mentoring program I was leading, we held a brainstorming session with both women and men. The goal of the session was to identify some common problems and then come up with real, actionable solutions. Everyone (men and women) was asked to write eight problems they'd seen affecting women in eight minutes, each problem written on a different sticky note and put on the wall.

There were about eighteen women in the room, and a handful of men—but the men were senior leaders in the company and people who could make changes. Several of the men told me later how much it impacted them to see the wall fill up with all of the problems women faced. They'd had no idea. They immediately came up with ideas to confront some of the themes that were raised in the session, and how to better support the women in their groups, something that had just never occurred to them before.

As I was discussing the solution-oriented approach I was taking to the women's mentoring program with Joe, he expressed that he wanted to help. I recapped some of the central themes, and specifically the point on sponsorship, and how "women are over-mentored and under-sponsored."

Joe said, "What if we just align these women with the senior leaders in my practice? What if I hold them accountable to sponsor the women?"

We went through the roster of the women at the senior manager level who were on the cusp of pushing into the executive ranks, and we paired them up with the most senior leaders in his group, about 90 percent of whom were men, to be their sponsors.

But I knew that wouldn't be enough. The men didn't know the issues that women faced, so wouldn't know what to look for or how to help the women.

To combat this, we invited the women and their newly-assigned sponsors to come to a workshop. The workshop agenda was simple. After I introduced the goals of their sponsorship, and the goals for the workshop, a few of the women would tell stories about some of the ways unconscious bias or other factors had impacted their careers. Then, we would discuss as a group ways of addressing the issues. We wanted the conversation to stay oriented around action and solutions.

The session was illuminating.

When I introduced the session, I cited a study that was reported on NPR[6] that a startup company was so eager to eradicate the pay gap between men and women that they published the equation they used to calculate salary, essentially, it was experience multiplied by role and location.

What they found when they analyzed the results was that the gap between men and women didn't improve; it actually got worse. After they analyzed the data, they found it was because men overstated their experience, while women tended to be accurate or underreport. On the NPR report, they actually said men "lied" about their experience. I softened this by saying, "overstated." So, for the exact same amount of true "experience," men were getting paid more because of how they had reported their own experience upon joining the company.

While I told that story, the men in the room all nodded and the women's jaws dropped like, "Are you kidding me?" It was starkly obvious in the room how true the report was just by the way everyone reacted to it.

This made it immediately obvious that there needs to be a lens through which to evaluate those kinds of experience and performance statements to balance them out, otherwise, it will appear that a man has done more, but it's just the way he's reporting it versus how a woman would.

The rest of the session was just as illuminating, with women telling their stories of having to do the administrative work, or their work being undervalued compared with their peers.

Most of the men, to their credit, sincerely wanted to help the women succeed and had no idea that the women were facing these obstacles.

While I would like to give you a miraculous report that all of the women were promoted, the reality is that the whole company reorganized shortly after the initiative. The reorganization shuffled everyone so that many of the women and senior leaders were no longer in the same practice, and Joe moved to a different area of the company as well.

But I do believe that the men who participated in that workshop and who took an active part in those women's careers, had a step-change in their level of understanding of the playing field and empathy for the women playing on it.

Getting everyone to understand the challenges women, and other diversity groups face, and getting the men aligned to help right the field is critical.

## stop it when you see it

While the mentoring program I ran was more focused on experienced women, the reality is we need to start leveling the playing field the moment people walk into the workforce.

I was the session lead for a class of new joiners. Volunteering to teach in our corporate courses was common and encouraged, and a change of pace from project demands. Most courses last just a week or two. While many of them have now moved to be virtual, prior to the pandemic, they were a great way of networking.

As the session lead, I oversaw two classrooms, with about thirty students in each. The majority of the new joiners were straight out of college and around twenty-two years old. But there was also a group of about fifteen former military veterans.

The rooms were arranged with five or six people at a table, with six tables per room. At each table there was one woman or two at most. During an exercise, each table had to brainstorm the answer to a scenario and write it down on a big piece of butcher block paper. I was moving between the rooms monitoring the progress of the scenario. In both rooms I saw the same thing: At each table, the women were writing on the butcher block tablet, while the men watched and provided their opinions. Despite there only being one woman at each table, they were the ones who had the pen. There were only two tables out of twelve where one of the men was doing the writing.

I stopped both classes and highlighted what was happening. You may think, "Who cares, it's just an exercise." Yes, and if that were the only time I had seen women doing the administrative work in my career, I might not have stopped both classes to talk to them about it. You could see the women dropping their pencils. They didn't realize what they were doing either, or how it could impact them in the future.

I offered to host an optional women's discussion after class, designed to address women's issues, but I made sure that both women and men were invited. I had about twenty people come after class, and it was about 60/40 women and men. I explained some of the common obstacles and unconscious biases that women could face, like doing the administrative tasks as we'd just seen. One of the men asked, "If we see that on our projects, what can we do?" I was so happy the men were there and eager to learn and help change the game.

I said: "If you see that the women are being asked to take notes or set up meetings, suggest doing it as a round-robin where people take turns doing those tasks." I don't want the men to be unfairly burdened by doing the tasks either, and I would much rather those tasks be shared equally.

I also said that when they (both men and women) become bosses someday, they need to be aware of these tendencies, and make sure to give meaningful, content-rich roles to incoming new women equally to new joining men, and share the administrative tasks across men and women.

## supporting other diversity groups

While I focused on gender diversity, because that's where I have experience, I believe that many of the same principles could be applied to diversity of all types.

Listen and learn what factors impact each diversity group—each group will have different biases to overcome.

The only way to understand what the diversity group faces is for the leadership to listen to them.

Also, get leadership aware and engaged to support and sponsor that diversity group. Diversity group to diversity group mentorship is good but not sufficient; you need sponsorship from the leadership outside of the diversity group.

As we have seen, sponsorship is absolutely critical for a leader's career progression, and perhaps even more important for women and other diversity groups.

Networking can also be critical for a leader, both for growing a circle of influence and getting sponsors, but also for getting support for their team.

## NETWORKING

Networking is one of those words that is thrown around all the time, as if it's a given, as if everyone agrees that it's a good thing. But let's start with what networking is, and why it can be a good thing.

Networking is simply meeting or connecting with other people, outside of the traditional work environment. It is often done at work-sponsored or industry events like happy hours, workshops, or conferences.

Networking is all about expanding your circle of contacts. Networking may give you an opportunity to meet a senior person who may be able to serve as a sponsor to help you get to the next level. "Managing Your Career" explores the importance of making sure that people who are part of the committee making decisions about your career know the work you're doing. A networking event may also be a great way to meet those senior-level committee members and either introduce yourself or provide an update on what you've been working on.

You may also be able to find people who can help you with a current challenge at a networking event, or you might meet some eager employees who are a perfect fit for an open role.

Networking goes both ways, of course. While you may be looking to expand your circle of acquaintances, others will also be trying to network with you. You need to offer the same opportunity to those junior to you.

Networking can be hard for many people. It can feel awkward. I'm an introvert and I found networking to be very challenging for me. I'm very comfortable in my element and can act bold and in charge with my team. I also had no problem facing off with clients. But put me in a networking happy hour with a bunch of people that I don't know who aren't on my team, and I will be tempted to huddle in the shadows as long as I can.

My advice to you is that others will be out there networking. They will be getting sponsors and connecting with the people on the promotion committees. Don't be the person that doesn't. I wouldn't have been sponsored by Joe without networking.

Women tend to network less than men, so if you're introverted and a woman like me, you may have to grit your teeth and force yourself in the door. But do it. If you want to grow your career, get out there and meet people.

## more than a transaction

I also found that networking could be very transactional, and surface-level.

In order for networking to be effective, you need to build real relationships. If you're not doing that, networking is irrelevant. I don't know how many people came up to me during happy hours and introduced themselves and then went on to the next executive. I didn't remember them; I probably never saw them again. And I don't think I was uniquely forgetful; I think that's the norm for executives. Networking at happy hours is extremely challenging for both the junior and the senior people to create anything lasting.

So, how do you make the most of a networking opportunity? Here are couple of ideas and examples:

I met one individual at a networking event who has since become a colleague and friend. Cindy said hello to me, but she went well beyond that. She looked me in the eyes, and said her name, and made me say it back to her so I wouldn't forget. She was bold, bright, eager, and I never forgot her. I worked with her on a project shortly thereafter and she was as bold and energetic on the job as she was in the happy hour. So, if you're going to meet people at happy hours, be interesting, be memorable. Ask interesting questions, tell interesting stories that make the executive remember you and want to work with you.

If you are going to a networking event, it may also help to have a goal in mind. I once went to a networking event solely to get three minutes with my boss in person. It was just past Covid, and I'd been assigned to him during Covid, so we'd only met over video or in large group settings. I was hoping to get a few minutes with him. I met with others there but he was my focus for the evening. When he left, I grabbed my coat and left the event, too, "running into him" on the street and getting the chance to talk to him while he waited for his taxi. For me the event was a success because I had a single goal.

Maybe there is someone you want to meet, maybe there is someone you want to ask a question of. The more you know who will be at an event, the better you can be prepared for how you want to take advantage of it. And then be interesting and be memorable.

Another idea is that many corporations offer volunteer opportunities—join one of those events, and you may be able to work alongside an executive. When you're working together and collaborating, you'll be better able to meet the executive as an individual and have greater potential for building a real relationship.

Networking, to me, is only valuable if you can build, or at least start, a real relationship. If you're just collecting names or shaking hands but not making a lasting impression, networking is about as relevant to your career growth as bar hopping. It can be a powerful element and a piece of the puzzle for managing your career. You can use it to expand your network or talk to people who you don't normally have access to, so that they understand what you're doing.

The wider your circle, the more you're able to let them know what you're doing. After all, if you're working hard leading teams, you have to make sure you're getting proper credit for it.

## TAKING AND GIVING CREDIT

Shouldn't a good leader give credit to their team? From Jim Collins' book, *Good to Great*, Level 5 Leadership essentially says that the best leaders give the credit to their teams and take blame on themselves. I don't think it's a dichotomy. If a team is doing well and getting results, there is plenty of credit to go around. The leader can both give credit to the team, as well as take credit for the leadership of the team. I think it's a "Yes, and."

### it's about the team

You need to give credit to the team for all of their hard work. That's 100 percent true.

We had been working on a very large deal for a very long time. The client had announced that we'd won the deal months earlier, but because of the complexity and size of it, it took months to do the contract. When the contract was finally signed, we all expected the congratulatory note to come out from the boss. But it didn't. We had lots of work to do to get the program started, so everyone kept their nose to the grindstone, but we were all still waiting for the email.

I asked the boss if he was going to send it. He said, "I feel like there has already been so much press on this deal that no one wants another email." He was feeling awkward and didn't want to toot his own horn again.

I said, "A lot of people have joined the program since those initial emails went out, so they weren't part of them. And it is good for the team to get the email to thank them for all of their hard work over the past weeks and months on the contract and on getting the program initiated. And, all of those people are waiting for that email so they can forward it on to their mentors and practice leads."

The boss was so embarrassed to send an email again that he forgot the main point, that it wasn't about him. His team needed the email, his team wanted him to thank them and to see the fireworks going off after all of their hard work.

He sent the email and thanked me for pushing him to do it.

## many (most?) leaders are still interested in career growth

Yes, and . . . since many leaders want to keep pushing up in the ranks, they also have to make sure their own leadership contributions are noticed and acknowledged.

A leader can both give credit to the team, as well as take credit for themselves, but the leader needs to do it in a way that the team doesn't feel slighted or like the leader is taking credit for their work. In my opinion, the best way to balance that is to have multiple messages for different audiences.

As an example, on Project Blast, on the morning of our go-live event that Friday, two days before the mandatory five-month launch date, I had several emails queued up to send.

The first email was to the clients to announce the site was live. This first message thanked the clients for their partnership and for the opportunity to do the work. The team leads and my bosses were copied on the email. There were plenty of emails from the clients back to us, and from the bosses to the clients congratulating the clients and the team. Everyone knew the clients were on that email, so the clients and the success of their new site was the focus of the email.

The second message was to the full team, copying all of our leadership. This email was entirely focused on the team and the work they'd done to pull off a miracle. I thanked them for their long nights and creativity and made sure all of the leadership knew how much of a miracle it was. There were a ton of reply-alls from the leadership on the email, and that was the email that each of those individuals would send to their practice leads and mentors and bosses. That message was entirely focused on the team.

I wrote a third message to my bosses and the board leaders who had supported me. I thanked the bosses and board of directors for their support, but I also wove in all of the gymnastics I'd needed to do to get the site launched. I didn't copy anyone from my team on the third email, and it was my way of making sure no one forgot the work I did when end of year performance reviews came around.

Each of the messages had a very different purpose. If I had tried to blend them, it wouldn't have been right.

The clients needed to rave and cheer about the launch of the site.

The team needed to feel celebrated and to get all of the kudos from the leadership.

A separate note allowed me to make my points to my bosses about how hard the project was and how much I had to do to make it work, without taking anything away from the team.

I also think that the team is well aware of how much their leader has contributed to the success of the team. For the leader who is engaged and present and helps the teams address challenges and provides the air cover from bosses and stakeholders, their team will happily share credit with them. The team will equally know when the leader is taking credit they haven't earned.

## taking credit where it's not deserved

Leaders taking credit for the work of others is another thing entirely, and when it happens, it can sour the relationship between the team and the leader.

On Project Falcon, I mentioned the client who, after our successful Labor Day weekend merging of the two systems said, "That's leadership," as if somehow he deserved all of the credit. (He deserved none of it, in my opinion.)

Similarly, his boss, the VP of the IT organization for Project Falcon, did a presentation at an industry conference about the lessons learned from doing the system merge. He took all of the credit for our work and didn't mention my team or the consulting firm. We had even built the PowerPoint presentation for the conference and coached him through the talking points.

As consultants our job was to make our clients successful, and we were paid to do that job, so I can understand not using the company name in the conference. But he didn't even show up that weekend to thank the team for all of their hard work nor praise the team in the office. That was taking credit for work that wasn't earned, and that wasn't leadership.

The other broad example of people who take credit where it's not deserved are those who excel at "managing upward," as I have mentioned before. Those people who manage upward often are experts at positioning themselves. They are adept at making it seem they are running things, but in reality they are standing back and letting others do the hard work, sidestepping if things look like they may fail, and stepping forward if there will be a success. Again, that's not leadership. The team will notice even if the leadership fails to.

In addition to giving and taking credit, the leader must be able to both provide and receive feedback. Feedback should, of course, be both positive and constructive and is critical for career growth.

In my opinion, "constructive" feedback is the most important and must be given thoughtfully in order to help guide each individual's career growth.

## GIVING FEEDBACK

Giving feedback should be one of a leader's favorite activities, because it allows one to focus on and mentor an individual and help them reach their career goals. What could be more rewarding for a leader?

The reality is that giving feedback is sometimes a chore that leaders avoid. Why? Because not everyone is a star performer and it's sometimes hard to give critical feedback to those who need to make significant improvements. Sometimes leaders don't like giving those messages that can be perceived as negative or harsh.

Even for the star performers, maybe especially for them, everyone has areas to improve on if they are going to grow their career.

Here's the thing about giving feedback: It's not about you. Feedback is all about the person being reviewed, so the best thing to do is focus on them and what they need to do to grow. Your goal should be to give fair, specific feedback that will enable them to grow to the level of their ability. If you are truly focused on the individual, your own potential discomfort should fade into the background.

As a leader you'll want to receive feedback as well; we'll discuss that too, whether that feedback is from your bosses or stakeholders or from your team.

## we all want feedback

Not only does everyone need feedback; everyone wants it too, even the "constructive" kind. Early in my career, I was promoted to the next level and then made to be the supervisor to someone who had previously been my peer, Lisa, who was and is still my friend. Lisa and I had arrived at the project the same day; we shared an office, and we shared all of the ups and downs of the job.

Because of my experience from the military, I was up for promotion earlier than she was. But the reality is we joined the consulting firm at about the same time, so being made her "supervisor" and having to write her end of year feedback made me very nervous. It was also my first feedback form in the civilian world. I didn't want to lose a friend, but I wanted to do my job well.

I wrote the feedback and was as fair and honest as I could be. At the time, our review format included a mandatory "areas for development" section, which meant there would always be some suggested improvements, no matter how much of a rock star someone was.

Our policy was also to walk the person through the feedback, rather than just submit it to their file, which I believe should be the standard for every company. Because I was so nervous to provide feedback to her, we went to lunch and I brought the feedback with me. I thought the informal environment might make the discussion easier.

Lisa took the form, scanned the "achievements" section in about half a second, and immediately focused on the "areas for development" section. I had included a few points that she should focus on, which would help her in the long run. She read that section completely and then looked back up at me, ready for the discussion.

I said, "You didn't even look at the 'achievements' part."

Lisa said, "I know what I did. The 'areas for development' section is the important part."

She appreciated the feedback and agreed with the points I'd made. We had a great discussion and I've always thought of that first feedback session as a model for doing reviews. Because she was my friend, I wanted to be extremely fair, while giving her the feedback that I felt she needed to advance her career. Treating all reviews with that level of care, while focusing on the individual and what they need to grow, should be the standard.

As I received and gave reviews in the future, I noticed myself and others looking straight at the areas for development, to see where we needed to improve, just like Lisa had done that first session.

If you need to give feedback to someone who is genuinely not performing well, and if they have not had a chance to shift to a different role, here are a couple of key points to keep in mind:

**Not giving proper feedback will not help, and may be harmful to someone's career.** A woman in my practice (but not on my team) was getting negative reviews on her project, and I was so surprised by it that I spoke to her supervisor on the project. She was in an entry-level role, but when her boss asked her to do something like make copies or put data into a spreadsheet, she would decline and say her supervisor should do it instead. That was mind-boggling from an entry-level person. She'd gotten into her mind that she should be doing strategy work and thought that anything else was beneath her.

I called the supervisors from her two previous projects and asked if they had seen any of the same kind of behavior. Yes, they both said, without hesitation. The first project had taken an opportunity to roll her off because of her attitude, but hadn't given her the specific feedback verbally, and hadn't written anything down in her feedback form, so she was unaware of how her attitude was impacting her. Their excuse was they weren't sure if that behavior was a trend for all new joiners, and they didn't want to hurt her career. The second project did essentially the same thing—found an excuse to roll her off quickly without telling her why.

At this point, the entry-level person was floundering on her third project, and no one had sat down with her and told her the real reasons. I had to give her the feedback, but she didn't believe it because neither of her last two projects had said anything.

Instead of being "kind" to the person by not giving her a specific constructive review, they allowed her misconceptions about what work aligned with her "talents" to continue unchecked. We started the process to fire her from the company, which is unusual for entry level, but she quit first. If she had gotten strong feedback at the first project, she might have been able to adapt and grow with the company.

**Start by asking the person how they think they did.** If you believe the feedback discussion is going to be challenging, ask the person how they think they did. In my experience, the vast majority of the people on the team know exactly how they're performing. They'll know some of their own areas of improvement and maybe even be harder on themselves than their supervisor would be. If they acknowledge their own challenges, the discussion will be less confrontational and more about what they can do to improve.

The most challenging discussions will be those people for whom there is a wide divergence between what they believe about their own performance, and your view. They may perceive themselves as the lynchpin of the organization, when your view is the whole team had to surround that person to support their work, or that they just plain didn't meet objectives. Sometimes, even if you are giving feedback throughout the year, they just won't believe anything other than that they're crushing it. For those discussions, the more specifics you can have, the more you can have things documented, the better off you'll be.

**They should never hear something for the first time on a feedback form.** Especially if someone hasn't been performing well, they should be getting feedback throughout the year. They should be hearing both that they aren't living up to the expectations or meeting the objectives, as well as the things they need to be doing differently. The more they hear the messages, with genuine advice for improvement, the greater chance they have for improving.

**Provide specifics.** Feedback that is too general can be frustrating or be hard to address unless there are specific examples. If you tell someone they need better "communication skills," that can mean very different things to different people, so the more specific the example you can provide the better. Perhaps a recent presentation went poorly, or perhaps the person has a hard time rolling up the message into a tight executive-level summary on a PowerPoint. Maybe their emails sound too informal. Provide some guidance in terms of what you saw, and an example of what they could have done instead.

I was told once that I needed better "executive presence," which is a common area of growth for improvement as someone is advancing to the executive levels. I was given no specifics of what I wasn't doing. I was only told to watch a few of my mentors and see what they did. I read books on executive presence and tried to follow the principles from the books. When I taught a week-long course, I asked the course sponsor to provide feedback on my executive presence. He said I did fine and didn't give me any specifics either. Because I was never given any specifics of what I wasn't doing, I always felt like I was chasing a ghost and never knew if I had achieved "executive presence."

**Tell them what is holding them back, even if you think they can never change it.** Arturo was a strong architect, very technical, and understood the system we were working on better than anyone else. He was greatly respected in the organization as an architect. He was a senior manager trying to push for those executive levels.

Joe came to do a review of our project—that was the first time I met him. In a one-on-one discussion he asked me how the team was doing. I ran through a list of the team leads, telling him who was performing well, who I might have to roll off. When I came to Arturo, he said, "He will never be promoted if he can't write a proper email."

I knew what he was talking about. Arturo's emails were informal at best, illegible at worst. Arturo had come to the US as an adult and he had a heavy accent in his speech. In his emails, his English grammar was challenged to say the least. But it wasn't just that. It was that Arturo dashed off emails as if he were writing long texts, using acronyms and abbreviations, and not using capital letters or punctuation. And while it might possibly be appropriate to use that style of email with his team, Arturo used the same "style" no matter who he was writing to, whether to the boss, Joe, or to his team members or the client.

If Arturo was to be promoted to the next level, Joe was right, he could never send an email like that to a CIO or a client executive.

After Joe left, I sat Arturo down and gave him the feedback. He needed to write business-appropriate emails if he was ever to be promoted. I promised to work with him and provide coaching both on the style, as well as to help improve his English grammar.

Over the next few weeks, for every email I got from him, I sent back all of my red-lined corrections and suggestions and talked him through my corrections to make sure he understood. Shortly after that I was moved to a different project and I stopped receiving emails from him because he was no longer part of my team.

After about six months, I was copied on an email from him and I had to check and double check who the sender was because it looked so entirely normal, so business-like, with perfect English grammar. It seemed like it was written by a different person.

I immediately forwarded the email to Joe to make sure he'd seen the turnabout in Arturo's style. It should no longer be seen as an inhibitor, and it could only help his chances for promotion.

Joe's reply was immediate. Joe was as amazed as I was at the turnaround. Joe had never once told Arturo that his email style and poor grammar was holding him back because he never thought Arturo would be able to make the change.

Even if the change will be hard for a person, even if you think they'll never be able to achieve it, tell people what they need to do to improve. You may be surprised what people can do when they're motivated.

## recurring meeting

The same way that I advocate for a recurring meeting with your clients or bosses, I believe that having a recurring meeting to discuss performance is useful. It has to be a meeting dedicated to performance otherwise, there are usually more pressing topics about the work which will take all of the time.

On some projects, I had my direct reports set up 30/30 with me, which are thirty minutes every thirty days.

Every time we had one of those meetings, I was always amazed by how rich the conversation was. Knowing the meeting was coming up on my calendar, I might jot down a few points regarding what the individual had done in the past month, both the good and things for which I could provide some constructive insight. We might also talk about what their next role might be, or if they have the right sponsors and mentors.

I found that having the dedicated time on the calendar was more effective than someone just asking me for feedback out of the blue. In those cases, I rarely had anything to say. It was too sudden, and I needed to think more and provide feedback more thoughtfully.

These recurring meetings allowed me to incorporate all of the points we've just discussed, from focusing on the individual to providing feedback that will help them grow, no matter how hard it might be for them to change. It also enabled me to make sure that feedback was covered in person prior to it being in an end-of-year report.

It also helps to build a relationship and builds trust. The individual will see through the time you're giving and the thoughtful feedback you provide how much you are invested in their career growth.

Obviously, you may not be able to do this for everyone on your team, but for those top direct reports who are pushing for the next level, it's vital. You can also change the frequency, even thirty minutes every quarter is better than not having a dedicated time to talk.

As a leader, you also need to receive feedback, both from your team and your Stakeholders.

## receiving feedback from stakeholders

In order to receive timely and thoughtful feedback as a leader, you should set up the same kind of recurring meeting with your boss or stakeholder. They are also busy and may not think to give you feedback unless you ask for and are given time for those kinds of meetings.

Listen to the feedback that is provided with openness. Feel free to ask clarifying questions, but don't slide into defensiveness or they may be less likely to provide feedback in the future.

Have your own questions ready, such as whether you performed well on specific areas where feedback would be helpful, like presentations.

I also recommend bringing a point of view on your own performance or career growth, such as, the next role you're considering or senior leader you'd like to meet with for their guidance.

While your stakeholder is the one providing feedback, getting that feedback is such a crucial element for your growth that you want to be prepared for it. First by getting it scheduled, and second by having your own thoughts or questions ready.

## feedback from the team

We have touched upon getting feedback from the team in various ways throughout the book. The key requirement of getting valuable (and honest) feedback from the team is to build relationships and trust with them. A team member is not likely to give you any direct feedback if you haven't earned their trust; they may be afraid you could use it against them later.

Even then, I have found that except for your most trusted lieutenants, or those you have the strongest relationship with, it may be awkward for a team member to give direct feedback to the leader. A more effective mechanism may be to ask feedback about the team, which indirectly provides feedback on your leadership. And even then it may still be awkward for people to answer directly.

What I found was the most effective way to get feedback about the progress of the team, or about things I should be focusing on, was to hold sessions with a handful of team members at a time, sometimes over lunch or coffee. At the sessions, I would ask everyone to say one thing they liked about the team and one thing they would improve about the team. And then we would do one fun fact about each person to make the discussion more fun.

I would often volunteer to start, unless someone else was willing. Having everyone provide both a positive point and a "constructive" point, removed the awkwardness of me asking directly for feedback on the team. And I always learned a ton of things about different people's perceptions of the team. I made sure that everyone on the team was invited to a session, which enabled me to hear from everyone and removed a possible perception of favoritism.

Feedback is a crucial element of being a leader and for helping your team manage their careers. As a leader you need to make sure you're both giving thoughtful feedback and getting as much feedback, both from your team and your stakeholders, as possible.

# 6.

# LAST POINTS

As if leadership isn't challenging enough, not only do you have to accomplish the WHAT of your objectives; not only do you have to take care of your team and create the working environment by HOW you lead; not only do you have to take care of your team's careers and manage your own; but on top of all of that, you may have to work in an evolving work environment where your team is no longer gathered around you.

## REMOTE WORK

The evolution of the work environment might find you in a remote or hybrid situation. Or, even if you work in an office, your team may be distributed globally.

Connecting to your team remotely introduces new challenges for a leader. The pandemic changed a lot of our expectations about work. I, along with many other leaders, got the opportunity to experience leadership through the screen of a laptop and it required a paradigm shift.

I started on a huge new Mega Program called Pyramid during the pandemic. It was a very large multi-tower project and despite being in the company over twenty years at the time, because of some shifts in our organization I didn't know a single person on the project. I had to lead teams and make relationships, all behind my computer screen.

There are a lot of articles about whether organizations are as productive working remotely or not, and there is still a lot of debate. I think how productive a team is depends on whether a team is starting up remotely versus being an already-established team continuing to work in a remote environment.

For the existing, well-oiled team, the reduction in hours spent commuting can increase the focus on getting the job done. People can roll out of bed, get coffee made, send their kids off to school, open the laptop, and know what they have to do to be productive.

But for new teams, or new joiners who don't understand the company culture yet, getting a new team to feel like a family and "firing on all cylinders" is extremely challenging. People may not know each other so trust and engagement is likely lower. Getting people to join "fun" or team building exercises remotely is another burden in their already video-meeting filled day. They may not know what they need to do to be successful or productive and training is more challenging because you can't just sit with someone and watch what they do over their shoulder.

If you are put in the position of having to build a strong team while being remote, below are a few factors to consider.

**You only hear what you are being told.** On both Project Blast and Project Ascend, I sat in the middle of the team area, and being in the middle of the team allowed me to overhear conversations and adjust where needed.

It also gave the team the opportunity to raise their hands if they wanted to help with something, like on Project Blast when Melissa asked to help with training after she overhead me interviewing a training expert.

In the remote work environment, there is no more "overhearing" other people's conversations. The only thing you hear is what you're being told. And sometimes what you're being told may not match the reality.

On project Ascend, I had a project manager act and talk like he was the best project manager ever. But because I sat in the war room with the team, I watched him pontificate about his greatness all day and not do any actual work. His team was struggling and he was sitting and spouting nonsense. I rolled him off and his replacement was 1,000 percent better.

But if I'd met him in a remote world, it would have been harder to determine if he really was the knight in shining armor he professed to be, or if it was a facade and he was just good at managing up.

While pre-pandemic I considered myself to be very good at judging people's contributions to the team, in the remote world it became harder to be certain.

**You don't spend time with the junior levels.** In a remote environment, as the leader, you will tend to be on meetings and video calls only with the next level of leadership and won't have as much interaction with the more junior members of the team.

Interacting with the junior members of the team can be valuable for several reasons. First, I find that there are some amazingly talented people in the junior levels, and I like to make sure they're being fully challenged so they'll stay engaged. I also like to mentor those levels as they can grow into the best managers and leaders.

I also find that the junior levels will sometimes have great insights into what's going well and what needs to get fixed on the project. But they'll only confide those things with you if they trust you and if they have a relationship with you. Being remote limits the ability to build those relationships with the junior levels and get those candid discussions.

You may need to be creative to create meeting opportunities for the junior members of the team. Create a program where a few junior members at a time are invited to participate in leadership meetings, so they can learn. Use the time to learn from them, at the same time as they're learning. Or, create skip-level meetings, where the leader meets with junior employees without their direct reports. Or, create a coffee-corner informal meeting where anyone on the team can join to ask questions or hear the latest update. There are lots of ways to connect with the junior levels, but in a remote environment, it will likely take more planning and forethought.

**Go on camera.** When I joined Mega Program Pyramid at the start of the pandemic, no one was on video. The screens were dark, and since I had never met anyone on the team, I felt blind.

I flicked my camera on. Even if I was the only person on video, the team was going to know me.

The principle of reciprocity is strong in video-calling. If one person is on video it is very hard for others to stay hidden behind their dark screen. After I turned my camera on, a few others popped their cameras on. And it makes a difference. You know who you are talking to. You learn their mannerisms and you see their expressions. You build relationships.

Of course, as I have no poker face, I was given feedback after that project by both bosses and clients that I should stay *off* video, especially if I was upset. But for me, I'd rather they know how I'm feeling. If I'm happy or engaged or upset, I'd rather they know it. And I'd rather know how my team or my clients or my bosses are feeling.

Video isn't 100 percent as effective as being in person with someone, but it's certainly better than being on a blank phone call with no idea who you're talking to.

**Get people together, or travel if you can.** Even if you're in a remote environment, if it is possible to travel to meet people, or to get people together in person occasionally, it's worth the effort and cost.

On Mega Program Hydra (pre-pandemic) I started interacting with my client in Belgium on the phone, and for the first couple of months it was very challenging. There was an accent, and we were dealing with complex topics. When I finally went to Belgium to meet my client Randy, I realized there was also a huge dose of humor and sarcasm in everything he said, which I hadn't been able to pick up on through the accent over the phone.

After that first time meeting Randy in person, every time I spoke to him, I was able to understand where he was coming from, understand what was humor and what was real. We developed a very solid relationship, even though I would only go to Belgium every few months. Having been there, I was able to process his voice and understand him so much better.

In another example of the value of getting together in person, in 2022, I traveled to India to meet our team. It was the first time I'd traveled to India since the pandemic. I knew that in the US many people were still not coming back to the office— but the impact of the pandemic on work from home in India was even more stark.

In cities like Bangalore and Mumbai, after the pandemic had forced everyone to work from home, no one was eager to return to the office because commutes can take up to two hours each way because the traffic is so atrocious. When I went to India, the whole team came to the office to meet me. It was, shockingly, the first time that almost everyone on the team had met each other, after over a year of being on the project. They hadn't been in the office and only came in because I was there.

We had an All Hands Meeting, did a brainstorming session on how to improve some challenges we'd been seeing, and did all of the things that used to be "normal" in the office.

While I was there, one of the leads pulled me into a room and told me how the junior leader that I'd brought in to manage the team day-to-day in the US was so harsh he was making people cry, and how many of the team were threatening to quit.

I felt like I'd been punched. Not only because I had worked so hard to get this team working well together and I hated the thought of anyone negatively impacting the team, but I also felt bad because I'd had to fly all the way to India for them to tell me, while I'd been on video with the team in India at least weekly. The lead said it was a recent development, and since they knew I was coming they figured they would just wait to tell me in person. But I wondered if that was true. Would they have told me at all if I hadn't been there?

Making relationships and having hard conversations, those things are better in person versus video, no matter what. If you can get your people together or go meet your team, do it.

As a leader, taking care of your team may be more of a challenge in the remote environment. It may be harder to detect if people's engagement is lower, or if the team isn't gelling the way it needs to. As a leader in a remote world, it may be harder to take care of your troops but it still has to be done if you want the team to gel.

However, while "troops eat first" should still be the focus of a leader, don't forget that you have to take care of yourself as well. That is a lesson that frankly took me too long to learn.

## TAKE CARE OF YOURSELF

"Troops eat first" doesn't mean "only troops eat." You still have to make sure you take care of yourself.

It took me three months of being retired from my company to see how burned out I had been.

When I made managing director, my mentor, Marty, told me that being an executive was a marathon, not a sprint, and I had to pace myself. The funny thing is marathons are hard. Anyone who applies that analogy to living the corporate life probably hasn't run a marathon.

I ran one marathon, once. I wanted to get in shape, and being a goal-oriented person, I wanted a deadline, an objective I could strive for. So, I trained for a marathon.

I was never a runner. I had been a gymnast. Gymnasts usually only run the 30 feet to the vault, or the 10 feet into a tumbling run on floor. I'd had to run at the Academy but I ran just enough to make it through basic training and to pass the annual athletic test.

So, I prepared for the marathon. I cut a marathon training calendar out of a runner's magazine and followed it religiously.

The night before the marathon I registered and got my runner's number, my T-shirt, and the map of the course. I considered driving the course to familiarize myself with it. But I thought, *26 miles, that's a long way, I don't have time for that!* And then I realized I will be running that distance!

Twenty-six miles is no joke. For me, it was 4 hours and 5 minutes of straight running, only taking a break around the 22nd mile to massage a huge cramp out of my thigh. My goal was 4 hours, and I was super happy with my 4 hour, 5 minute finish.

But here's the thing, marathons are long and unless you're a super marathoner and extremely in shape, they're hard on the body. By the end of the marathon, you're spent. My muscles were so sore, I was walking with a stiff-legged limp for the next couple of days.

Our careers should not feel like a marathon; that's not a good analogy. Our careers should not feel like we can't ever stop and can't ever take a break unless we have a massive cramp, and where we are so depleted afterwards that we walk with a limp for days.

When I left my career after twenty-five years, I looked back on it and realized I'd been running a marathon, and it had been hard. And I limped through the first couple of months of retirement trying to recover.

I was a poster child for not taking care of myself. I would be the first one into the office, so that I could get a few things done before everyone came in, which allowed me to spend the rest of the day focused on the team and on the clients. Depending on the project and the commute time involved, I was usually in the office by 6:30 or 7:00 in the morning. I once sat outside a client's office in the hallway at 6:30 in the morning, waiting for him to come in so that I could escalate an issue that happened over night. One of my clients would call me at 6:30 in the morning to talk through things because he knew I'd be heading into the office then.

I used to say: "If you stay plugged in, you never have to recharge your batteries." It was a joke, but not.

I left vacations early to attend meetings and missed some friends' weddings because I couldn't get away.

A colleague of mine, Brenda, used to ask me for advice related to work-life balance. She was a level junior to me, a few years younger, and she had younger kids, so she thought I might be able to help her through some work life balance challenges.

But she quickly stopped asking for my advice, because my answer was usually the opposite of what she was thinking. And my advice usually focused on getting the work done.

She said once that her husband had to get up early on Thursdays so he was always in bed by 10:00 p.m. on Wednesdays so . . .

I finished her sentence: "So you can stay up and catch up on work and not bother him."

She finished her sentence: "So I know I'll go to bed on time at least one night a week."

We looked at each other, and both shook our heads. I think that was the last time she asked my advice on work life balance.

Here's what I learned from the marathon:

## take real breaks

Leaving from a vacation early was *never* worth it. I did it twice in my career.

The first time, my boss decided he didn't need me in the meeting after all. They held the meeting that I'd flown home from California to attend, without me. I can't tell you how upset I was. I *can* tell you that no one did anything for me; no one even apologized.

The second time, I wanted to attend a client meeting remotely. But my boss said it was *critical* for me to be there in person. This was a *big* meeting, with a major opportunity riding on it. I agreed to fly home. But as soon as I got home, it snowed, and the client decided to do the big meeting remotely. I could have attended the meeting remotely from my vacation. Instead, I'd missed out on time with my family in order to do a one-hour remote meeting and then shovel snow.

I started traveling internationally partly as a defense against getting pulled back into work or getting guilted into returning to the office early. If you're in Nepal or Poland, it's a lot harder to come back to the office than if you're still in the US. Time zone differentials and availability of Wi-Fi and connectivity also limit how easy it is to jump on a conference call or review a contract. As soon as we felt our son was old enough for foreign travel (at around ten years old), almost all of our vacations were in a foreign country. Yes, I also love international travel, but being less accessible was a huge factor for me.

## build personal events into your schedule

Don't think you can multi-task personal events. If a call is running over and you have to leave for your event, leave. Tell everyone ahead of time you have a hard stop at that time, and leave, even if the call is running over.

You obviously will need to be thoughtful about which events you need to attend because you can't do that every day. But events you miss (or aren't paying attention to because you're on an urgent call) don't come around again. That friend's wedding or your child's birthday, those only happen that one time.

Go, and be present.

## give yourself time to think

At one point in my career, I had an executive coach. I had an hour-long session with her every week where I reflected about how the previous week had gone, and what was coming up. She coached me to think through the best ways to handle some challenges I was facing.

After the six-month session with her ended she encouraged me to continue self-coaching. She had given me such great advice and asked me such great questions that at first I was stymied by what I could do on my own that could be as valuable.

Then I started writing an email as if it was to her, though with no expectation of hearing back from her. Writing it "to" my former coach kept her voice in my head and allowed some of her coaching to still come into my subconscious.

I set aside an hour each week, usually on Fridays, and wrote a very simple email each week. I had three or four key sections:

What Went Well
What I Could've Done Better
What's Coming Up

Sometimes, I added what I'm grateful for, which I found really helpful to think about.

It was a very simple format, but I would spend the full hour writing the email, and the exercise forced me to think about my performance, what I needed to do, and how to prepare for the week ahead.

The exact questions you ask yourself, and the method you choose, maybe you prefer a notebook versus an email, are up to you. But I found that having time set aside to reflect was crucial to my growth. I also found that period of reflection to be very calming and helped me put the week in perspective before the weekend.

## if you have nothing left, you have nothing to give your team

You just don't. Do what you need to rejuvenate yourself.

For me, it was always travel. After Project Blast, I took myself to Sweden and Denmark and solo traveled for ten days until my mind and body started to recover.

After Project Ascend, I went to Japan and soaked myself in the hot waters of onsens until the nastiness of the project drained away.

Of course, I could only travel a couple of times a year, so I had to find small ways to rejuvenate every day. When I was on remote assignments, I loved reading over dinner and preferred eating by myself to eating with the team. While going out with the team was sometimes nice, I had focused on the team the whole day and really needed the quiet in the evenings. In every city I traveled to for work, I found a few restaurants that I loved and would go there any night I could.

I don't have answers for how to balance your life. I don't think anyone can tell you what is right for you. What I can tell you is you have to find something that works for you and put barriers up to protect it. You have to set some boundaries, or at some point you'll either have a massive cramp in your thigh and have to stop and work it out, or you'll run to the end and have nothing left to give.

# 7.

# SUMMARY

I spoke before about how leadership is waged on two dimensions, both the WHAT and the HOW.

The JOB you do will ultimately be judged by whether you accomplished the WHAT.

As a leader, your CAREER will ultimately be judged by the HOW.

As a leader in my company, I worked on many systems, building them from scratch, upgrading them, or maintaining them. But let's face it, technology changes quickly. Which means that many of the systems I built over my career are obsolete and replaced. Those that continue to run have gone through multiple upgrades since my team worked on them.

I spent twenty-five years of my life building systems only to see them replaced. Isn't that depressing?

No, the technology was never the point. In fact, most objectives you accomplish as leader aren't that relevant. There is always another sale, another case, another product. Those objectives are your JOB, and you need to accomplish them, but there will always be another objective coming.

As a leader what really matters is the team, the people you supported and influenced through all of the projects. What matters is the impact you had on the people on your team, those who you helped along the way. What matters is HOW you led and HOW the team accomplished the work.

All of the challenges and successes we just spoke about throughout this book, and how I reacted to them as a leader, were teaching and shaping the team, just as they taught me. Did I blame or did I solve? Did I leverage and support my team so they could be as successful as possible? The people on my team will carry those lessons forward into their next projects, into their careers, into the teams that they lead. They will try to replicate the strong bonds of family that they felt, like we had in Project Ascend where everyone was singing karaoke and gathered around the dining table in one of our teammates' hotel suites.

My team. Those people. They're my legacy. HOW I led them; that's my career, not the systems we built.

When I was retiring from my company, I told one of my former team members from Project Falcon that I was leaving. He was in India at the time of the project, but he had since moved to the US. He turned his video on and pulled my Guiding Principles card out from his wallet, where he'd carried it for twelve years. He said he had been continuing to use those same principles on his teams ever since.

At my retirement party, he gave me a mug with those Guiding Principles printed on it. I loved the mug, yet how much more meaningful is it to know that those Guiding Principles are still living on in his teams? He could not have given me a more meaningful gift.

As leaders we are in the people business. We lead people, and our most important output is people's skills and careers. If you impart even a few lessons to them that they carry forward into their careers, count your leadership as a success.

You need to accomplish the WHAT for your day-to-day job, but your legacy will be judged by HOW you led and HOW you treated and grew your team.

Lead following your guiding principles.

Lead from wherever you can be most effective.

Lead by remembering that your team, your troops, come first.

# APPENDIX

**Business/Consulting Terms**

**All Hands Meetings:** A meeting for all members of an organization.

**Death march:** An unending slog of work, including nights and weekends to get the work done at all costs.

**Deliverables:** Anything that has to be completed, such as documentation, code designs, or code.

**End users:** The people who will actually use a system, like call center workers who will use a call center application or salespeople who will use a sales tool.

**Fixer:** A leader who focuses on fixing "recovery" projects.

**Governance:** The set of meetings and materials by which a project is governed, usually including lower-level detailed meetings, as well as senior-level decision and status meetings.

**Managing up:** The set of actions that you need to do with your bosses or stakeholders, including such activities as communicating status and progress, requesting help, and representing the project's people in feedback and promotion discussions.

**Minimal viable product (MVP):** The minimal level of functionality necessary for a system or website, assuming that additional features will be added later.

**Production systems:** Systems that real-life users like call center agents use, versus copies of the systems that are used for testing.

**Project versus program:** A program is comprised of many projects.

**Recovery project:** A broken project, or a project that needs to be fixed.

**Release:** When code that has been developed is put onto the production systems.

**Resource:** shorthand for a Human Resource, or a person.

**Roadmap:** A list of features with a proposed timeline for post-launch release.

**Root Cause Analysis (RCA):** A detailed analysis of the root cause of a problem, especially when an incident has occurred. Up to seven levels of "Why?" are asked to get inside the heart of the challenges.

**Roll off (rolled off):** Leaving a project while still being employed and able to move to a different project.

**Stakeholder:** Any leader with a vested interest in the project or work you're doing, including clients, bosses, or leaders from related organizations, etc.

**Steering Committee Meeting:** A senior-level meeting designed to monitor the progress of the project and make relevant decisions when necessary.

**Socialize:** To review material with people prior to a meeting so they aren't surprised by anything at the meeting.

**Tribal knowledge:** A common term for knowledge gained over many years but not documented.

**User acceptance testing (UAT):** Testing completed by end users on a system prior to it being put into production.

**Military Terms:**
**Air Base Ground Defense (ABGD):** Defending Air Force Bases using Army infantry techniques.
**Launch Control Facility (LCF):** Literally houses the facility where missiles can be launched from. Missile launch officers man the post 24/7 in case there is ever a need.
**Non-commissioned officer (NCO):** Military leaders who have enlisted, and have not gone through college. By contrast, Officers must have a college education.
**Patrols:** When a squad of eleven or so people walk through the woods or the jungle to look for and defend against the enemy.

**Project List:**
**Project Falcon** was a large software development program with two different technologies.
**Project Ascend** was a project with two major workstreams, which included the work of a subsidiary company "SubCo" and which had been running for three years.
**Project Blast** was a lightning-fast project with just five months to launch a brand-new Cloud Native website with strong cyber-security.
**Project Nebula** was a major initiative to transition a Product from being on server-based hardware to being modular and dynamic - essentially a precursor to Cloud technologies.
**Mega Program Hydra** (pre-pandemic) Included six pillars, essentially running the majority of a company's IT department, as well as conducting major projects.
**Mega Program Pyramid** (launched during the pandemic) was a major program with multiple workstreams.

# ENDNOTES

1. There are mixed reviews of using the term "family" at work. While some are positive on it, as I am, some feel it may set up false expectations for the team. For more, see: Joshua A. Luna, "The Toxic Effects of Branding Your Workplace a 'Family,'" *Harvard Business Review*, October 2021, https://hbr.org/2021/10/the-toxic-effects-of-branding-your-workplace-a-family
See also: Nancy Solari and Micah Zimmerman, Ed., "3 Reasons Treating Your Team Like Family Is a Win-Win for Everyone," *Entrepreneur*, August, 2022, https://www.entrepreneur.com/leadership/how-treating-your-team-like-family-is-a-win-win-for-everyone/432962.

2. Michael Norton, "The IKEA Effect: When Labor Leads to Love", *Harvard Business Review*, February 2009, https://www.hbs.edu/ris/Publication%20Files/norton%20HBR%20the%20ikea%20effect_8f7edd3f-2f93-4544-a792-48a5ddf87664.pdf

3. "Why are New Professionals so Reluctant to Lead" https://www.google.com/url?sa=t&source=web&rct=j&opi=89978449&url=https://www.navalent.com/resources/blog/reluctant-leader/&ved=2ahUKEwj8gtGu7YGJAxXCkYkEHR7LLhUQFnoECBwQAQ&usg=AOvVaw1b7Oup96EE5BOPWfM17bgB

4. Irina Ivanova, "Why 'I quit' comes soon after 'you're promoted'—and companies keep bungling the career advancement process," *Fortune*, September 2023, https://fortune.com/2023/09/09/quitting-after-promotion-job-mobility-resignation/

5. Herminia Ibarra, Nancy M. Carter, and Christine Silva, "Why Men Still Get More Promotions Than Women," *Harvard Business Review*, September 2010, https://hbr.org/2010/09/why-men-still-get-more-promotions-than-women?referral=00134.org

6. David Burkus, "Would Work Improve If You Knew What Your Colleagues Get Paid?" NPR, *TED Radio Hour*, December 1, 2017, https://www.google.com/url?sa=t&source=web&rct=j&opi=89978449&url=https://www.npr.org/transcripts/567520005&ved=2ahUKEwiqp7PCgoKJAxXSK1kFHbLRGBYQFnoECBoQAQ&usg=AOvVaw0QZzebTOSRkUR9bVBgEqGW

# AUTHOR BIO

Tauni Crefeld, a graduate of the United States Air Force Academy, served as a Security Police Officer, where she applied leadership theory and gained practical insights by listening to her troops and attending US Army training courses.

After her military service, Tauni joined a major consulting firm, where she spent 25 years, rising from entry level to Managing Director. Known for turning around underperforming teams, she not only led them to achieve objectives but also focused on building cohesive, high-performing units.

Tauni and her husband have one son and a cat and live in New Jersey. An avid traveler, she has visited 75 countries and enjoys outdoor adventures with her family, including hiking, paddle boarding, rock climbing, and bike packing.

Made in the USA
Middletown, DE
06 February 2025